WALKS IN THE
YORKSHIRE DALES
BOOK TWO

30 SHORT CIRCULAR WALKS
OF
OUTSTANDING BEAUTY AND INTEREST

JACK KEIGHLEY

BOLTON PRIORY

WALK 44

WALKS IN THE YORKSHIRE DALES BOOK TWO

an illustrated guide to thirty walks
of outstanding beauty and interest

by

J Keighley

CICERONE PRESS

MILNTHORPE, CUMBRIA

ISBN 1 85284 065 X

Also by *JKeighley*
WALKS IN THE YORKSHIRE DALES
ISBN 1 85284 034 X   *Contains Walks 1-30*

INTRODUCTION

The area known as the Yorkshire Dales is many things to many people, but above all it is magnificent walking country. Walking has traditionally been the favourite pursuit of those visiting a region which offers a range of attractions perhaps unrivalled anywhere else in the whole of Britain : -

- wild, desolate fells
- extensive tracts of heather moorland
- rugged limestone scars, pavements and spectacular cliffs
- awe-inspiring caves and potholes
- deep river gorges and sparkling mountain streams
- exquisitely beautiful waterfalls
- green fertile valleys and flowery meadows
- outstanding views
- a vast network of public footpaths and bridleways
- remote, picturesque villages and bustling market towns
- ancient abbeys, churches and castles
- relics of ancient civilizations

The happiest person in the Dales must be the walker who is also a geologist. The major part of the area lies on a platform of ancient rock – chiefly granite – known as the Askrigg Block. Apart from a few isolated exceptions, however, this base platform lies covered by strata of more recently formed rocks, and of these it is limestone which dominates the geology, and consequently the scenery, of the Yorkshire Dales.

The Great Scar Limestone is up to 400 feet thick in parts of the western and southern Dales, and is magnificently exposed in Ribblesdale, Wharfedale and Malhamdale. Here, above the glistening cliffs and scars, are vast areas of limestone pavements weathered from the exposed blocks of rocks. About half the limestone pavement in Britain is found in the Yorkshire Dales. The Great Scar Limestone has not only undergone surface erosion, but is also honeycombed with complex underground cave systems. This is probably the finest caving area in Britain. The ordinary walker, who is too faint-hearted (or sensible?) to venture into these dank and sinister caverns, can safely sample the wonders of the underworld at three public show caves - White Scar Cave (Ingleton), Ingleborough Cave (Clapham) and Stump Cross Caverns (between Grassington and Pateley Bridge).

In the more northerly dales, notably Wensleydale and Swaledale, the Great Scar Limestone lies hidden beneath layers of rock strata known as the Yoredale Series. Formed in an alternate succession of sandstone, shale and limestone (of a darker kind than the Great Scar variety), the Yoredales have weathered to produce hillsides with a distinctive stepped profile.

In all parts of the Dales the highest fells are capped by beds of hard, coarse millstone grit.

Though nature has lavishly contributed this fine scenery, it is the influence of man which has helped to create the unique Dales landscape which we see today. The mineral resources of the region have been exploited for many centuries. The Romans are known to have mined lead, and this industry developed until, at its peak in the nineteenth century, thousands of miners, chiefly in Swaledale and Wharfedale, were employed in extracting and processing lead. The ruins, levels, hushes and spoil heaps of these old mines still remain – stark and grim and desolate.

Since the discovery that grassland was improved by the application of burnt limestone (hence the profusion of old lime kilns), limestone working has developed into a major Dales industry, and today high-quality limestone is quarried in several areas – most notably at Cracoe and Horton-in-Ribblesdale.

In the eighteenth century certain changes in the country's social and economic life had a marked effect on the Dales landscape. Between 1780 and 1820 successive Enclosure Acts led to a re-distribution of land and the construction of thousands of miles of drystone walls in the valleys and up the fellsides. This was an important building period in the Dales, and many of the present farms, cottages and barns are of that vintage. The Dales in fact have been inhabited since pre-history, and current walkers' paths date from earliest man to the drovers'and packhorse routes of the last two or three centuries. Many of these ancient green lanes still provide superb routes over the hills from dale to dale.

The other great influence on the landscape has been the grazing of sheep. The Dales are renowned for sheep, and years of careful breeding has produced animals which are ideally suited to the terrain and climate. Most popular is the famous blackfaced 'Swaledale', with its curly horns. The Yorkshire Dales National Park Authority has chosen the Swaledale tup as its symbol. Sheep-grazing has a profound effect on the natural vegetation of the area.

My purpose in writing this introduction has been to attempt a general description of the superb countryside which the lucky user of this book may expect to enjoy, and the major factors which have shaped and fashioned it. My sincere wish is that you may derive as much pleasure from these walks as I have had in compiling them.

J Keighley
March 1990

6

ABOUT THIS BOOK

THE WALKS The walks are numbered 31-60 as a continuation from the thirty walks contained in 'Walks In The Yorkshire Dales', the first book of the series. All the walks are circular, and begin at a place where a car may be parked without causing an obstruction. They are fairly uniform in length, an average of 6½ miles making them half-day rather than full-day excursions. Whilst several of the walks - those to the south and east in particular - lie outside the boundary of the Yorkshire Dales National Park, they are all within an area which the author regards as being of 'Dales Country' character. By this criterion the southern Howgill Fells have been excluded, as geologically and scenically they belong more to the Lake District. The selected walks collectively incorporate every type of landscape to be found in the Yorkshire Dales - riverside meadows, natural woodland, planted forest, limestone karst and gritstone moorland. The routes are almost entirely public rights-of-way, with occasional recourse to commonly-used tracks in open country. They should be free from serious difficulty, and well within the capability of reasonably fit and agile walkers.

THE MAPS The strip-maps show all relevant route-finding features. All the routes have been walked and surveyed in detail by the author, and great care has been taken to ensure accuracy, although for the sake of clarity there is deliberate distortion of scale in depicting routes along, for example, narrow lanes. Changes, however, will occur quite frequently, particularly on low-level routes, where the walker may expect to encounter new stiles and fences and sometimes diversions, either temporary or permanent. In such cases please note and obey any legitimate waymarks and signs. In the Route Directions any mention of a gate or stile means that it is used, unless otherwise stated. The maps and route directions should suffice to guide all but the totally incompetent (who in any case will have failed to locate the starting point). Nevertheless it is strongly recommended that an Ordnance Survey map be carried, as this will add interest and enable the walker to identify distant features not mentioned in the text.

7

WALKING IN THE DALES
A FEW WORDS OF ADVICE

- Many of the routes in this book cross agricultural land, and farmers will not welcome inconsiderate visitors. When crossing fields keep closely to paths, and walk in single file across meadowland. Avoid climbing walls, and securely close all gates behind you, unless they are obviously meant to be left open.

- Leave no litter.

- Dogs must be kept on a lead in the proximity of livestock. This is especially vital during lambing time (March to May).

- Cars must not be parked where they obstruct field gates or cause damage to grass verges. Lock your car securely and hide from view any attractive or valuable items (or take them with you).

- A few of the walks in this book begin at places known as 'honeypots'- which means that they attract large numbers of visitors and parking may be difficult. Try to avoid these places at weekends and Bank Holidays, or, if this is not possible, aim to make a very early start. The walks which particularly fall into this category are Nos 37 (Malham village), 50 (Kettlewell), 52 (West Burton) and 54 (Keld).

- When walking along a motor road walk on the right to face the oncoming traffic. The exception to this is on approaching a blind bend, where it may be necessary to cross to the left for a clear view.

- Before setting out, try to let others know where you're going.

- If the weather turns nasty, don't hesitate to call it a day and return by the route along which you came. Conditions in the Dales, particularly on the high fells, can change very quickly.

CLOTHING AND EQUIPMENT Boots or strong, comfortable shoes are essential (on the high fells and in winter boots are the only suitable footwear). A windproof jacket or anorak (preferably with a hood) will be needed. Thick, heavy sweaters are not recommended – two or three lightweight layers are warmer and more adaptable to changing conditions. Avoid jeans - they are not at all suitable. In cold weather a woollen hat or cap will prevent the loss of a great deal of body heat.

A rucsac is needed - a small 'daysac' with a capacity of about 20 litres would be adequate for any of the walks in this book. The author's rucsac will always contain the following items : —

- waterproof cagoule and overtrousers
- spare woollen pullover
- small first - aid kit
- large - scale O.S. map
- compass
- whistle
- plastic bottle for water or cold drink
- a high - calorie snack (usually chocolate or crisps)
- windproof lighter for getting the old briar going (the alternative being about 10 boxes of matches)

To these basic items may be added, as the occasion demands, a flask containing hot coffee, soup or a beef drink, a pair of gloves and a torch (for poking around in caves).

CHILDREN   When taking children on country walks some thought must be given to the distance and the type of terrain involved. Until you are sure of the child's capabilities, keep the distances short. Most of the walks in this book would probably be too much for a child under the age of five. As a rough rule of thumb, a child should be able to manage about a mile for each year of his age after his fifth birthday. Children should be warmly clothed and well shod. One cannot always afford to buy expensive boots for growing feet, but at least the child should have strong shoes or close - fitting wellingtons. On no account should young children be allowed to wander off beyond the range of vision of responsible adults, and extreme care and control must be exercised in the vicinity of crags and potholes.

9

THE WALKS

No		MILES	No		MILES
31	RAMSGILL AND LOFTHOUSE	5	46	COLSTERDALE	6¼
32	CAPPLESTONE GATE	5¾	47	FREMINGTON EDGE AND ARKLE BECK	7½
33	WILLANCE'S LEAP	5½	48	THE ASCENT OF WHERNSIDE	7½
34	EMMERDALE FARM COUNTRY	5¾	49	HARKERSIDE MOOR AND APEDALE	8½
35	LECK FELL AND EASE GILL	6	50	KETTLEWELL AND STARBOTTON	5
36	JERVAULX ABBEY	6¾	51	ILKLEY MOOR	6½
37	MALHAM COVE AND NAPPA CROSS	5	52	FORELANDS RIGG	5¾
38	CAVES AND POTHOLES OF BIRKWITH	7	53	THE ASCENT OF BUCKDEN PIKE	7½
39	THE ASCENT OF GREAT HAW	6	54	KELD WATERFALLS AND WHITSUNDALE	7¼
40	LOWER GARSDALE	6	55	BORDLEY TOWN	7½
41	LEYBURN SHAWL	6	56	PIKE HILL AND HARDRAW FORCE	7¼
42	BURNSALL, THORPE AND LINTON	5½	57	A CANALSIDE WALK FROM GARGRAVE	7
43	WHITE SCAR CAVE AND MEREGILL HOLE	6¼	58	AROUND BARBEN BECK	5
44	BOLTON ABBEY AND HAZLEWOOD MOOR	6¼	59	HARD LEVEL GILL AND GREAT PINSEAT	5½
45	CASTLE BOLTON AND CARPERBY	8¼	60	BEYOND MALHAM TARN	7½

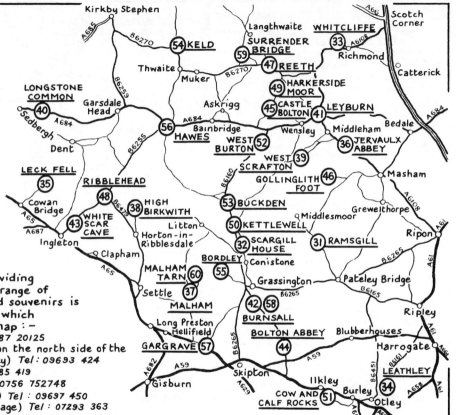

ROAD MAP

OF THE AREA SHOWING THE

STARTING POINTS

OF THE 30 WALKS DESCRIBED IN THIS BOOK

NATIONAL PARK CENTRES

There are six National
Park Centres within
the Yorkshire Dales National
Park, all aiming to enhance
the enjoyment of visitors by providing
advice and information. A wide range of
books, maps, posters, leaflets and souvenirs is
available at these centres, all of which
are in the area covered by the map :—
SEDBERGH (town centre) Tel : 0587 20125
AYSGARTH FALLS (in the car park on the north side of the
  river, off the A684 west of Wensley) Tel : 09693 424
CLAPHAM (village centre) Tel : 04685 419
GRASSINGTON (Hebden Road) Tel : 0756 752748
HAWES (in the former station yard) Tel : 09697 450
MALHAM (at south entrance to village) Tel : 07293 363

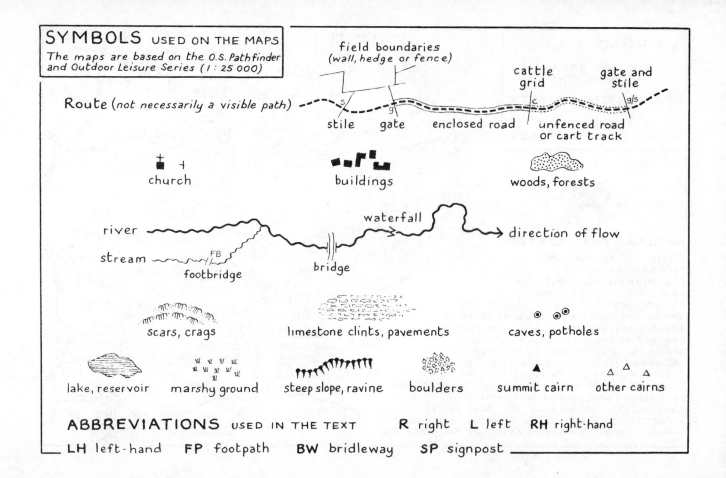

SYMBOLS USED ON THE MAPS

The maps are based on the O.S. Pathfinder and Outdoor Leisure Series (1 : 25 000)

field boundaries (wall, hedge or fence)

Route (not necessarily a visible path)

stile   gate   enclosed road   cattle grid   gate and stile

unfenced road or cart track

church

buildings

woods, forests

river

stream

footbridge

bridge

waterfall

direction of flow

scars, crags

limestone clints, pavements

caves, potholes

lake, reservoir   marshy ground   steep slope, ravine   boulders   summit cairn   other cairns

ABBREVIATIONS USED IN THE TEXT

R right   **L** left   **RH** right-hand

LH left-hand   **FP** footpath   **BW** bridleway   **SP** signpost

RAMSGILL
& LOFTHOUSE

5 MILES

From Ramsgill - as pretty a village as you could wish to see - this easy walk provides glorious views of the peaceful and attractively wooded upper reaches of Nidderdale. A very short detour will enable a visit to be made to the famous and spectacular How Stean Gorge. The walk is almost entirely along sections of the Nidderdale Way.

path by the wood
near Longside House

JKeighley

13

PARKING Cars may be parked on the green at Ramsgill, but only alongside the churchyard wall. *Map ref: 118 709*
If this is not possible there are alternatives at the Lofthouse end of the walk – a car park along the How Stean lane, a layby near the cricket field or a car park in the village near the Crown Hotel.

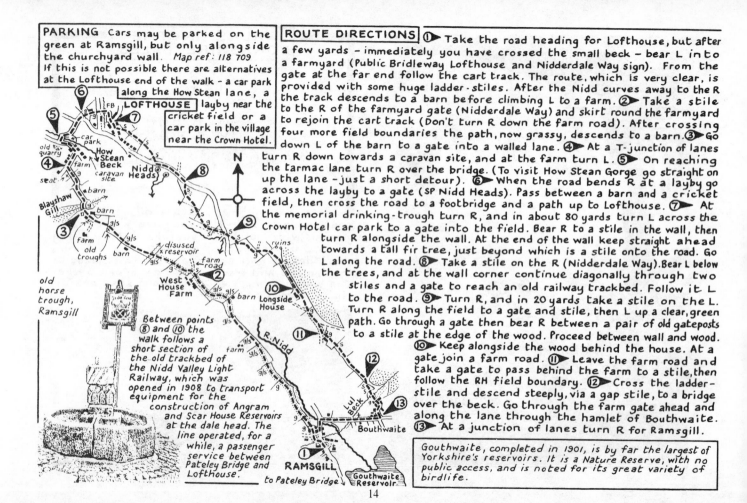

old horse trough, Ramsgill

Between points ⑧ and ⑩ the walk follows a short section of the old trackbed of the Nidd Valley Light Railway, which was opened in 1908 to transport equipment for the construction of Angram and Scar House Reservoirs at the dale head. The line operated, for a while, a passenger service between Pateley Bridge and Lofthouse.

ROUTE DIRECTIONS ① Take the road heading for Lofthouse, but after a few yards – immediately you have crossed the small beck – bear L into a farmyard (Public Bridleway Lofthouse and Nidderdale Way sign). From the gate at the far end follow the cart track. The route, which is very clear, is provided with some huge ladder-stiles. After the Nidd curves away to the R the track descends to a barn before climbing L to a farm. ② Take a stile to the R of the farmyard gate (Nidderdale Way) and skirt round the farmyard to rejoin the cart track (Don't turn R down the farm road). After crossing four more field boundaries the path, now grassy, descends to a barn. ③ Go down L of the barn to a gate into a walled lane. ④ At a T-junction of lanes turn R down towards a caravan site, and at the farm turn L. ⑤ On reaching the tarmac lane turn R over the bridge. (To visit How Stean Gorge go straight on up the lane – just a short detour.) ⑥ When the road bends R at a layby go across the layby to a gate (SP Nidd Heads). Pass between a barn and a cricket field, then cross the road to a footbridge and a path up to Lofthouse. ⑦ At the memorial drinking-trough turn R, and in about 80 yards turn L across the Crown Hotel car park to a gate into the field. Bear R to a stile in the wall, then turn R alongside the wall. At the end of the wall keep straight ahead towards a tall fir tree, just beyond which is a stile onto the road. Go L along the road. ⑧ Take a stile on the R (Nidderdale Way). Bear L below the trees, and at the wall corner continue diagonally through two stiles and a gate to reach an old railway trackbed. Follow it L to the road. ⑨ Turn R, and in 20 yards take a stile on the L. Turn R along the field to a gate and stile, then L up a clear, green path. Go through a gate then bear R between a pair of old gateposts to a stile at the edge of the wood. Proceed between wall and wood. ⑩ Keep alongside the wood behind the house. At a gate join a farm road. ⑪ Leave the farm road and take a gate to pass behind the farm to a stile, then follow the RH field boundary. ⑫ Cross the ladder-stile and descend steeply, via a gap stile, to a bridge over the beck. Go through the farm gate ahead and along the lane through the hamlet of Bouthwaite. ⑬ At a junction of lanes turn R for Ramsgill.

Gouthwaite, completed in 1901, is by far the largest of Yorkshire's reservoirs. It is a Nature Reserve, with no public access, and is noted for its great variety of birdlife.

14

Church of St.Mary the Virgin, Ramsgill.

The pride and joy of RAMSGILL is its large and picturesque village green, set in front of lovely old cottages and dominated by the ivy-clad Yorke Arms. The hotel was once a shooting-lodge owned by the wealthy Yorke family. The cottage next to the hotel was originally the village school. The church was built in 1842, on the site of a chapel built by the monks of Byland in the days long gone when Ramsgill was a grange of their abbey. At the north-east corner of the churchyard, incorporated into the wall, is the gable end of the monks'chapel. The nearby hamlet of BOUTHWAITE was a grange of Fountains Abbey. LOFTHOUSE, higher up the dale, is rather larger than Ramsgill, and doesn't have the same sleepy atmosphere. The War Memorial, in the form of a drinking-trough, has interesting words.

gable of old chapel

barn near Blayshaw Gill

Take a peep through the bottom LH door (no need to go inside) to see a really old, traditional Dales shippon.

At NIDD HEADS the River Nidd emerges from two caves (about 150 yds apart), having flowed for some two miles through the labyrinth of passages which make up the famous Goyden Pot system. The caves cannot be seen from the road, and cannot be entered without proper caving equipment. LONGSIDE HOUSE was formerly a Youth Hostel but was forced, for financial reasons, to close down in 1983.

O.S. MAPS :   Landranger Series (1 : 50 000) Sheet 99
(Northallerton and Ripon)
Pathfinder Series (1 : 25 000) Sheet SE 07/17
(Upper Nidderdale)

© Jack Keighley 1990

32

CAPPLESTONE GATE

5¾ MILES

Set in the heart of beautiful Wharfedale, this short walk embodies just about every typical feature of Dales country. Here are white limestone walls, pavements and gleaming scars, potholes, dark plantations, ancient packhorse routes, sombre gritstone moors and remains of old mining activities. Height is gained easily, and most of the walking is on dry, close-cropped turf.

JKeighley

O.S. column Capplestone Gate

PARKING Not easy in this area. Two roads connect Grassington and Kettlewell – the main B6160 via Kilnsey and, on the east side of the river, a narrow lane via Conistone. It is from the latter that the walk begins, and the suggested parking place is a small, triangular roadside recess about a mile from Kettlewell, just below Scargill House. The recess has two field gates (which must not be obstructed), a stile and a signpost (FP To Bycliffe Road 2)

Map ref: 976 708

In case of difficulty an alternative would be to park at Conistone (though here again parking space is limited). A walled track (FP Middlesmoor 11) from just north of the village joins the walk at point ③.

ROUTE DIRECTIONS ① Cross the stile at the parking place and set off up the broad cart track (known as Highgate Leys Lane). ② On leaving the wood at a gate and stile turn R off the cart track to follow the wall on the R. When the wall turns away to the R continue straight on, keeping to the R of a scar, to a ladder-stile. The way is now clear along a level limestone terrace via several ladder-stiles. ③ The Bycliffe Road, a broad stony track, is reached at a 4-way signpost. Turn L (FP Middlesmoor). ④ When the Bycliffe Road turns sharp R turn L through a gate into a field (FP Capplestone Gate). Keep towards the RH side of the field. ⑤ At the wall corner turn R past the end of a small plantation. The track climbs by the wall before swinging L to a gateway in the wall at the LH end of a scar, then bears R up to the O.S. column. ⑥ Cross the ladder-stile and turn L (FP Kettlewell). Keep a level course roughly parallel with the wall on the L. (Intermittent path with a few cairns). After crossing an area of mining debris *don't* take the ladder-stile on the L. Stay above the wall to reach another ladder-stile by a gate. ⑦ Cross this stile and descend steeply to a path running about 50yds from the wall on the L. (*For detour see notes on Langcliffe Pot*). The path curves R through a broken wall into a very long field. ⑧ The official right-of-way descends the field in a big, sweeping S-bend, but it is quicker, easier, and safer in mist or snow, to stay by the wall on the R. ⑨ From a gate about 50yds from the bottom of the field a clear track slants down to re-join the outward route.

to Kettlewell

Scargill House

The entire walk is accomplished without setting foot on tarmac.

slopes of Great Whernside

Langcliffe Pot

⑦

× ancient boundary stone (falling over)

⑨

shafts

⑧

to Conistone

Since 1959 Scargill House has been a C. of E. conference centre. It has a modern, and very prominent, Scandinavian-style church.

mine spoil

FOOTPATH TO MIDDLESMOOR

FOOTPATH TO CONISTONE

FOOTPATH TO GRASSINGTON

FOOTPATH TO KETTLEWELL

O.S. column
CAPPLESTONE GATE 1680'

⑥

plantation

Swineber Scar

limestone scar

clints

barn

plantation

⑤

signpost at point ③

N

Conistone Pie

limestone pavements

kiln

Hill Castles Scar

④

Bycliffe Road

③

Conistone (Scot Gate Lane)

On approaching point ④ look back for a view of the magnificent limestone pavements.

16

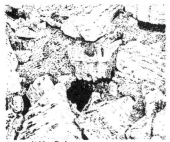
Langcliffe Pot

To see the notorious LANGCLIFFE POT a short detour is necessary from point ⑦. On crossing the ladder-stile turn R to follow a faint track along the west side of the wall. About 50 yds before reaching the crosswall turn down the slope to locate a shakehole with limestone blocks. Amongst these is a rather innocuous-looking hole, from which emanates the sound of flowing water. Do not, under any circumstances, venture into it, for it leads to a 90' pitch. The extensive system of underground passages is liable to flooding, and is regarded by potholers as one of the most difficult and dangerous in the country.

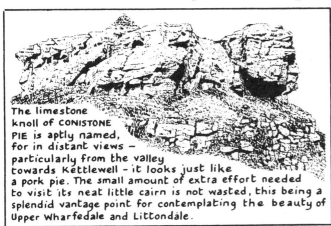

The limestone knoll of CONISTONE PIE is aptly named, for in distant views – particularly from the valley towards Kettlewell – it looks just like a pork pie. The small amount of extra effort needed to visit its neat little cairn is not wasted, this being a splendid vantage point for contemplating the beauty of Upper Wharfedale and Littondale.

O.S. MAPS : Landranger Series (1 : 50 000) Sheet 98
                              (Wensleydale and Wharfedale)
               Outdoor Leisure 10 (1 : 25 000) Yorkshire Dales
                                     (Southern area)

WALKS IN THE YORKSHIRE DALES

③③

WILLANCE'S LEAP

5½ MILES

A popular and easy walk in the richly colourful countryside immediately up-dale from the ancient and fascinating town of Richmond. The outward route traverses the edge of a long limestone scar, from where the views, both into Swaledale and east across the Vale of Mowbray, are truly magnificent. The return is along the wooded slopes below the scar.

Willance's monument

This tall, shapely cairn stands beside the farm track below Applegarth Scar.

PARKING Leave Richmond by the main Reeth road, but before reaching the edge of town, where the road bends L, keep straight on up a lane (Westfields). Park on the verge where the tarmac ends at a gate ('No Through Road' sign.)
Map ref: 153 015

ROUTE DIRECTIONS ① Go through the gate and along the farm road. ② On passing through another gate, by the farm, turn R (waymark) and climb the steep field, bearing L to reach a gateway in a fence. ③ Leave the track and bear L, keeping above a patch of gorse to come alongside a fence on the L. Follow it to a stile. ④ Beyond the stile the path continues along the top of the scar, with the fence now on the R. Near the monument a wall takes over from the fence and the path stays close to it, eventually swinging R to run above a deep valley on the L, before descending to join a motor road at a cattle-grid. ⑤ Turn L and walk along the road for almost a mile. ⑥ Turn L through a gate (Bridleway sign) onto a farm track. ⑦ At the farm ignore a path going down to the R. Stay with the main track as it passes in front of the house and then bears L. ⑧ Just beyond the farm leave the track and go to a waymarked gate by a barn on the R. Through the gate turn L and pass alongside the barn and forward on a level course through two stiles (with 'Coast to Coast' signs) to reach a tarmac farm road. ⑨ Cross the road to another 'Coast to Coast' stile and continue forward across two more fields to join a farm road. ⑩ Leave this road almost immediately in favour of a fence stile on the L, then continue forward alongside the road. Pass through a stile and follow a fence on the R to reach a broad track coming up from the farm on the R. ⑪ Go L along this track, passing through Whitcliffe Wood to emerge close to point ②.

The road walking between ⑤ and ⑥ is not unpleasant, being downhill and with lovely views into Clapgate Gill.

There are some fine YEWS along the route — massive, rather squat trees with gnarled and fluted trunks and foliage of rich dark green which appears almost black from a distance. The pinkish-red 'berries' are properly called arils, for they are cup-shaped and do not completely enclose the seeds, which lie at the base of the cup. The seeds are poisonous, as also are the leaves and the bark. Yews have a life-span of about 1000 years, and were once regarded as a symbol of everlasting life.

The walk from ⑥ onwards is practically level throughout.

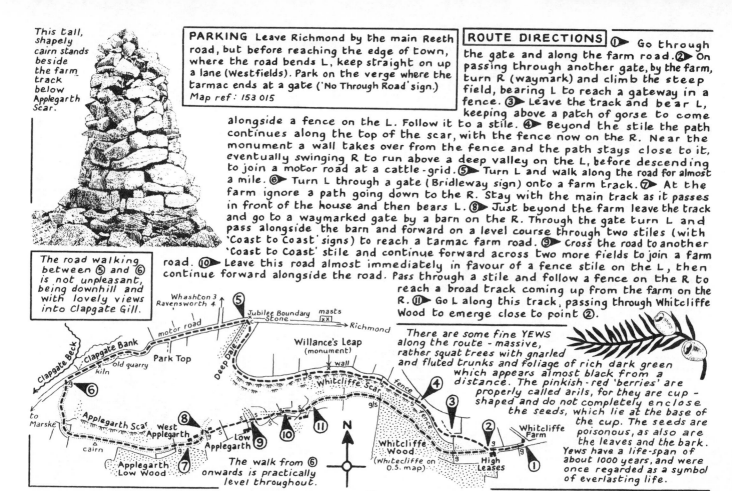

18

HEAR US:
GLORY BE TO OUR
MERCIFUL GOD
WHO MIRACULOUSLY
PRESERVED ME FROM
THE DANGER SO GREAT
○
THIS STONE WAS RENEWED
AD 1815
GEORGE SMITH ESQ MAYOR
○
AND
○
AGAIN RENEWED AD 1843
PETER CONSTABLE
MAXWELL ESQUIRE
MAYOR
○

In the autumn of 1606 Robert Willance, a local man from Richmond, was out with a hunting party when his horse bolted and leapt over the edge of Whitcliffe Scar. The fall of some 200 feet resulted in the death of the horse, but the rider miraculously survived. Two monuments commemorate the incident and record Willance's thanks to God. He also gave a silver chalice to the town.

In spring and early summer the hillside between High Leases Farm and Whitcliffe Wood is ablaze with yellow gorse – a most beautiful sight.

The road along which we walk between points ⑤ and ⑥ was the main Richmond to Reeth road prior to 1836, when the new road was built. It also serves as the National Park boundary, which at point ⑤ turns south along Deep Dale and cuts across our route at the first stile after point ⑧.

From Applegarth Scar onwards we are following The Master's footsteps, for this is a section of Wainwright's famous 'Coast to Coast' walk from St. Bees Head to Robin Hood's Bay.

O.S. MAPS : Landranger Series (1 : 50 000) Sheet 92
(Barnard Castle)
Pathfinder Series (1 : 25 000) 609 (NZ 10/SE 19)
(Richmond and Leyburn)
(Outdoor Leisure 30 contains all the route west of Whitcliffe Wood)

© Jack Keighley 1990

EMMERDALE FARM COUNTRY

5¾ MILES

A delightful ramble through countryside so peaceful and pastoral, and yet so close to the massive Leeds - Bradford conurbation, whose residents may find this an ideal walk for a summer's evening or a winter's afternoon. The route passes close to the 'Emmerdale Farm' of TV fame, and much of the location filming takes place in the area.

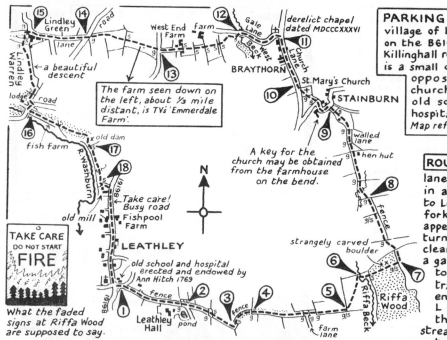

15 Lindley Green **14**

road

lane

Lindley Warren

← a beautiful descent

lodge road

16

fish farm   × old dam

R. Washburn   **17**

18

B6161

old mill

TAKE CARE! Busy road
Fishpool Farm

Take care! Busy road

What the faded signs at Riffa Wood are supposed to say.

West End Farm   **12**   Gate Lane   *derelict chapel dated MDCCCXXXVI*

West Beck

13

BRAYTHORN   Church Lane   **11**

The farm seen down on the left, about ⅓ mile distant, is TV's 'Emmerdale Farm'.

St. Mary's Church   **10**

STAINBURN

9   walled lane

hen hut

N

A key for the church may be obtained from the farmhouse on the bend.

8

fence

9/s

strangely carved boulder

6   **7**

5   Riffa Beck   Riffa Wood

LEATHLEY

old school and hospital erected and endowed by Ann Hitch 1769

B6161

1   fence   **2**   **3**   **4**

Leathley Hall   pond   fence   farm lane

carved boulder in Riffa Wood

PARKING   At the village of Leathley, on the B6161 Pool to Killinghall road. There is a small car park opposite the church, by the old school and hospital. Map ref: 232 470

ROUTE DIRECTIONS   **①** Set off along the lane opposite the church (SP Stainburn), and in a few yards turn R along the tarmac drive to Leathley Hall. **②** At the Hall, when the lane forks, keep L (straight on). **③** When the path appears to end abruptly at a gate in a fence, turn L to cross a stile in the same fence. A clear path beyond it climbs between trees to a gate. **④** From the gate go straight forward to join a wide track. Keep straight on, as the track heads towards a large wood. **⑤** Upon entering the last field before the wood, turn L and cross the field diagonally, aiming for the LH corner of the wood. **⑥** Cross the stream on concrete blocks by the fence and enter the wood via a stile. Go straight up the wood on an ancient paved path. **⑦** On leaving the wood turn L to walk alongside it. At the end of the wood bear slightly L up to a gate, pass through it and follow the fence on the R. **⑧** When the fence ends go forward on a broad green path, cross a small stream and follow the LH field boundary to the road at Stainburn. **⑨** Turn L, and at the lane's second bend turn R up to a small gate (public footpath sign). Go up to the church. **⑩** Turn R along the lane. **⑪** At the chapel turn L down a grassy lane. **⑫** Immediately after crossing a bridge take a stile on the L into the field. Climb the RH side of the field, and when the slope eases bear L to stiles in a double fence. Go straight on past a short wall to the farm beyond. Enter the farmyard by a step stile in the wall, and leave along the farm road. **⑬** Take the gate opposite the end of the farm road (public footpath sign). Cross the field past a solitary tree, and in the next field bear R to follow its RH boundary to the road. **⑭** Cross the road and go along the lane. **⑮** When the lane bends sharp R leave it to pass through a gate ahead (public footpath), and immediately turn L over a stile in a fence.

Go down through a gate in a wall and descend, on a clear path by a wall on the L, to the road. Turn R. ⑯ At the bridge go down steps on the L (public footpath) to a path alongside a tall hedge. At the end of the hedge cross a stile and continue on a clear, level path through trees, which eventually descends to the River Washburn. ⑰ Follow the riverside path downstream. ⑱ Use a stile on the L, near the roof of a shed, to pass round the buildings to the main road. Turn R for Leathley.

St. Mary's Church, Stainburn   derelict chapel, Braythorn

The village of LEATHLEY has a general air of affluence and some very desirable residences. The CHURCH OF ST. OSWALD dates from c.1100, and the Norman parts of the building include the tower, the east and west walls of the nave, the chancel arch and the west door and window. The west door is particularly ancient and has very interesting ironwork. The church was enlarged about the year 1472 by the addition of the aisles, and extensively restored about a century ago. The priest's stall, lectern, font cover and choir seats are all by Thompson of Kilburn, and bear his famous 'mouse' trademark.

O.S. MAPS :   Landranger Series (1:50 000) Sheet 104
               (Leeds, Bradford and Harrogate)
               Pathfinder Series (1:25 000) Sheet SE 24/34
               (Harewood)

35

LECK FELL & EASE GILL

6 MILES

A delightful walk up the lovely valley of Leck Beck to a tremendous limestone gorge. Set at the north-western extremity of the Dales, this colourful countryside is frequented more by potholers than by walkers, for beneath your feet is Britain's most extensive cave system. Yorkshire Dales scenery at it's best, as one might expect — it's in Lancashire!

Ease Gill Kirk   JKeighley

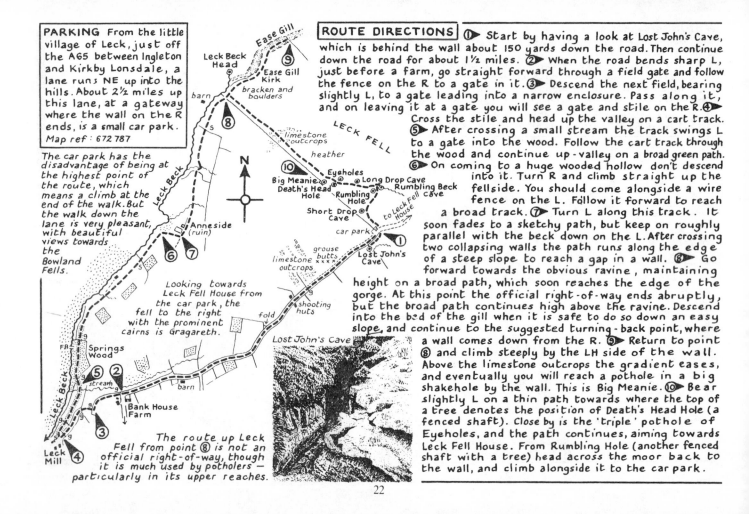

PARKING From the little village of Leck, just off the A65 between Ingleton and Kirkby Lonsdale, a lane runs NE up into the hills. About 2½ miles up this lane, at a gateway where the wall on the R ends, is a small car park. Map ref: 672 787

The car park has the disadvantage of being at the highest point of the route, which means a climb at the end of the walk. But the walk down the lane is very pleasant, with beautiful views towards the Bowland Fells.

Looking towards Leck Fell House from the car park, the fell to the right with the prominent cairns is Gragareth.

The route up Leck Fell from point 8 is not an official right-of-way, though it is much used by potholers — particularly in its upper reaches.

Map labels:
Ease Gill
Leck Beck Head
Ease Gill Kirk
bracken and boulders
barn
8
LECK FELL
limestone outcrops
heather
10 Eyeholes
Big Meanie
Death's Head Hole
Long Drop Cave
Rumbling Beck cave
Rumbling Hole
Short Drop Cave
to Leck Fell House
car park
1
Lost John's Cave
Leck Beck
N
Anneside (ruin)
6 7
grouse butts
limestone outcrops
shooting huts
fold
barn
Springs Wood
FB
5 2
stream
Bank House Farm
3
Leck Mill
4

Lost John's Cave

ROUTE DIRECTIONS

1 ► Start by having a look at Lost John's Cave, which is behind the wall about 150 yards down the road. Then continue down the road for about 1½ miles. **2** ► When the road bends sharp L, just before a farm, go straight forward through a field gate and follow the fence on the R to a gate in it. **3** ► Descend the next field, bearing slightly L, to a gate leading into a narrow enclosure. Pass along it, and on leaving it at a gate you will see a gate and stile on the R. **4** ► Cross the stile and head up the valley on a cart track. **5** ► After crossing a small stream the track swings L to a gate into the wood. Follow the cart track through the wood and continue up-valley on a broad green path. **6** ► On coming to a huge wooded hollow don't descend into it. Turn R and climb straight up the fellside. You should come alongside a wire fence on the L. Follow it forward to reach a broad track. **7** ► Turn L along this track. It soon fades to a sketchy path, but keep on roughly parallel with the beck down on the L. After crossing two collapsing walls the path runs along the edge of a steep slope to reach a gap in a wall. **8** ► Go forward towards the obvious ravine, maintaining height on a broad path, which soon reaches the edge of the gorge. At this point the official right-of-way ends abruptly, but the broad path continues high above the ravine. Descend into the bed of the gill when it is safe to do so down an easy slope, and continue to the suggested turning-back point, where a wall comes down from the R. **9** ► Return to point **8** and climb steeply by the LH side of the wall. Above the limestone outcrops the gradient eases, and eventually you will reach a pothole in a big shakehole by the wall. This is Big Meanie. **10** ► Bear slightly L on a thin path towards where the top of a tree denotes the position of Death's Head Hole (a fenced shaft). Close by is the 'triple' pothole of Eyeholes, and the path continues, aiming towards Leck Fell House. From Rumbling Hole (another fenced shaft with a tree) head across the moor back to the wall, and climb alongside it to the car park.

EASE GILL CAVERNS

Ease Gill is born high on the slopes of Great Coum, just to the south of Dent, and flows sedately down the peaty moor until it encounters limestone. Here it promptly disappears underground to flow through a complex maze of passages beneath a classic limestone gorge, uniting with streams from many other potholes in the area before powerfully re-emerging at Leck Beck Head. This magnificent cave system, with its winding streamways, huge waterfall shafts and vast caverns is a potholer's paradise, and contains some of the finest stalactite displays in the country. In times of severe flood, when the caves fill to overflowing, the swollen waters of Ease Gill come raging overland down the normally dry ravine

● ● ●

LOST JOHN'S CAVE is perhaps the best known in the area. It has two entrances (wet and dry) which unite inside, and can be explored by experts for a distance of over six miles. DEATH'S HEAD HOLE, which drops into a cavern 150 feet high, and RUMBLING HOLE are impressive open shafts. The water seen falling into Rumbling Hole is the stream which sinks at RUMBLING BECK CAVE some 60 yards to the north east. LONG DROP CAVE (at the bottom of a shallow dry valley) and BIG MEANIE both lead to big underground pitches. At SHORT DROP CAVE, a small hole which is also located at the bottom end of a small dry valley, a stream can be seen flowing along its subterranian channel only a few feet below ground level.

The ruins of Anneside

O.S. MAPS : Landranger Series (1 : 50 000) Two maps are needed – Sheets 97 and 98. Pathfinder Series (1 : 25 000) No 628 (SD 67/68) (Kirkby Lonsdale and Barbon)

36

JERVAULX ABBEY

6¾ MILES

An exploration of the atmospheric ruins of one of Yorkshire's great Cistercian Abbeys is followed by a delightful and easy ramble through parkland and pastures. The return is along the banks of the sparkling Cover and the sedate Ure. The walk is almost level, and yet is set amid undulating wooded countryside which provides scenery of the very highest quality.

Chapter House   J Keighley

PARKING Use the official Abbey car park (signposted) by the A6108 between Masham and Middleham. Map ref: 169 857

ROUTE DIRECTIONS ① From the car park turn L along the main road and in a few yards take a metal gate on the R. Follow the gravel path to the ruins. ② Return part way along the gravel path and turn L onto a wide drive through the park. ③ On leaving the park continue forward along a tarmac lane. ④ About 80 yds past the bridge turn L through a gate (the second of two large double gates). Go forward to another gate leading into a big field, and go straight across the field to a stile (marked with a white post) in the hedge. Go through a gap at the far RH corner of the next field and turn R to the farm. ⑤ Turn L at the farm over a stile (with white post) and follow path along edge of fields. At a stile in a wire fence near a copse bear ½ R to reach a hedge to the R of two large trees. Cross two narrow enclosures to a waymarked gate and a walled lane. ⑥ Turn L through the village and take a gate into the grounds of Manor House (SP road to St. Oswald's Church only). ⑦ When the road forks keep L downhill. ⑧ Cross the little car park to a gate and go straight on to a small gate in the field corner. Continue alongside the wall, at first on its L and then, after a stile, on its R. ⑨ Just beyond a small plantation turn L through a small gate and turn R to follow the top edge of the field to another gate. From here go almost to the wall of Danby Hall. ⑩ Join a wide cart track which heads away across the park. On reaching a gate by a cottage keep straight on along the farm road to join a tarmac lane (keep straight on). ⑪ At the T-junction turn L (E. Witton ¾) over the bridge. Turn L at the main road, pass the inn (unless it's open) and over another bridge. ⑫ Take a small gate on the L immediately past the bridge and follow the clear riverside path. ⑬ On reaching a cross fence turn R through a gate and up a cart track to the main road. Turn L.

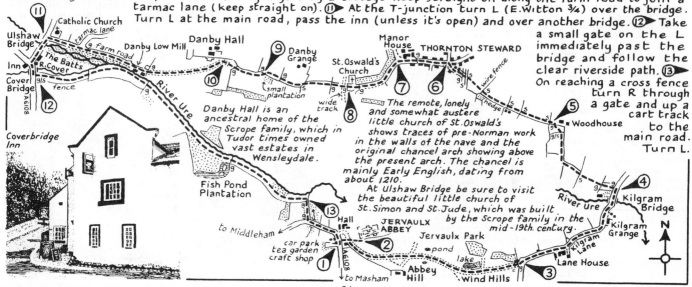

Danby Hall is an ancestral home of the Scrope family, which in Tudor times owned vast estates in Wensleydale.

The remote, lonely and somewhat austere little church of St. Oswald's shows traces of pre-Norman work in the walls of the nave and the original chancel arch showing above the present arch. The chancel is mainly Early English, dating from about 1210.

At Ulshaw Bridge be sure to visit the beautiful little church of St. Simon and St. Jude, which was built by the Scrope family in the mid-19th century.

Map labels: Catholic Church, Ulshaw Bridge, tarmac lane, Danby Low Mill, Danby Hall, Danby Grange, Manor House, THORNTON STEWARD, The Batts, R. Cover, Inn, farm road, St. Oswald's Church, wire fence, Cover Bridge, fence, River Ure, small plantation, wide track, Coverbridge Inn, Danby Grange, Woodhouse, hedge, Fish Pond Plantation, River Ure, Kilgram Bridge, to Middleham, Hall, JERVAULX ABBEY, Jervaulx Park, pond, lake, Kilgram Grange, Kilgram Lane, Lane House, car park tea garden craft shop, to Masham, Abbey Hill, Wind Hills

24

Jervaulx Abbey

was founded in 1156 by a company of monks who had forsaken a very bleak establishment near Askrigg in search of a more hospitable site. At the height of its power Jervaulx owned half of the valley of the Ure. It was particularly renowned for breeding horses, and its monks are thought to have invented the recipe for the original Wensleydale cheese. The last abbot of Jervaulx, Adam Sedbar, was hanged at Tyburn in 1537 for his part in the Pilgrimage of Grace. The abbey was severely mutilated, and very little can be seen of the great church which measured 270' by 63'. However, considerable remains of the domestic buildings survive. Look for the various masons' marks in the dressed stone, particularly in the Chapter House. About fifteen different designs are evident. The buildings and grounds are privately owned, and are open to the public during daylight hours. By the small gate at the south-west corner of the ruins is an honesty box for admission payment. Guide books and postcards can also be obtained here.

the village pump Thornton Steward

KILGRAM BRIDGE is considered by many to mark the eastern boundary of Wensleydale. It is an ancient bridge and a very fine one, with its six arches standing high over the broad river.
According to local folklore the bridge was built by the Devil in a single night.

O.S. MAPS : Landranger Series (1:50 000) Sheet 99
(Northallerton and Ripon)
Pathfinder Series (1:25 000) No 630 (Sheet SE 17/18)
(Middleham and Jervaulx Abbey)

© Jack Keighley 1990

25

37

MALHAM COVE & NAPPA CROSS

5 MILES

A grand walk in fine, open hill country. Although short, the walk is quite a strenuous one, climbing to the highest point around Malham at almost 1700'. Choose a clear day, and avoid weekends and Bank Holidays, when the village and The Cove (one of the most spectacular natural features in the Dales) will be seething with tourists.

JKeighley

limestone blocks above Malham Cove

PARKING Large car park (pay and display) at south entrance to Malham village. Map ref: 901 627

ROUTE DIRECTIONS ① ▸ Walk into the village, and at the centre keep straight on along the road signposted Malham Tarn 3 Langcliffe 7 Settle 8. ② ▸ About 100yds beyond the last house on the R (Town Head Farm) turn R through two gates (Pennine Way) onto the 'tourist path' to The Cove. ③ ▸ When the path forks take the L branch to a stepped path climbing steeply to the top of The Cove. ④ ▸ Cross the triple stile and turn R onto the extensive limestone pavement. At the far end of this you will come to a crosswall. Don't cross it, but turn L to follow it up the dry valley. ⑤ ▸ At the stile at the head of the dry valley keep straight on alongside the wall on the L. In about 50yds cross the wall at a ladder-stile (FP Langscar Gate ¼) and follow the wall up to the road. ⑥ ▸ From the gate across the road a Land Rover track winds uphill, keeping fairly close to the wall on the R. ⑦ ▸ On passing through a gateway the path forks. Take the grassy path climbing ½ L up to a gate and maintain direction through two more gates. From the last gate head L towards a post sticking up from the wall on the skyline (Nappa Cross). Follow this wall forward to reach a gate in it. ⑧ ▸ Turn L through the gate (SP Malham) and, on a clear path, descend to a guidepost where the path forks. ⑨ ▸ Turn R (FP Malham 1½ M) on a narrow path skirting limestone clints on the L. When the clints end the path virtually disappears, but keep straight on and, as the slope steepens, you will see a ladder stile in the wall ahead. ⑩ ▸ From the stile a sketchy path (waymarked with yellow blobs here and there) keeps fairly close to the limestone hillside on the L. (Ignore any tracks going off to the R across the gritstone moorland). Descend to another ladder-stile. ⑪ ▸ Aim for a barn, beside which is a ladder-stile, and from here bear slightly R towards another barn. ⑫ ▸ Turn L along a walled lane (SP Malham). ⑬ ▸ At a T-junction of lanes turn R to arrive at the car park.

old level below Pikedaw Hill

SOME ADDITIONAL NOTES : To locate THE GROLLIT from the second gate above point ⑦ bear ½ L for about 100yds to an area of clints and a small pool. The hole is covered by a heavy wooden pallet, which must be replaced. From hereabouts there is a beautiful view of MALHAM TARN. JUNIOR POT lies in a small shakehole (not easy to find) above the path some 100yds from the gate before Nappa Cross. LOW GRIT HOLE is in a shakehole 30yds to the R of the path, just beyond the guidepost. Approaching point ⑬ the green conical hill (reef knoll) ahead is CAWDEN.

Dean Scar
Langscar Gate
Comb Scar
⑤
⑥
⑦
limestone scenery nonpareil
The Grollit (pothole)
Junior Pot
④
THE COVE
NAPPA CROSS
Pikedaw Calamine Caverns
THE NATIONAL TRUST
MALHAM TARN ESTATE
③
clapper bridge
Malham Beck
Nappa Gate
Low Grit Hole
⑧
⑨
Miners' Hole
PIKEDAW HILL
level hillside
limestone hillside
②
gritstone
⑩
⑪
ford and slab bridge
Town Head
⑫
N
⑬
car park, toilets and Nat. Park Centre
①
MALHAM

26

ℵappa Cross

Nappa Gate stands near the summit of a bridleway between Settle and Malham which has been in use for many centuries. Re-sited prominently on top of the wall 200yds to the north are the remains of a wayside cross which is probably of monastic origin. During medieval times Malhamdale west of Malham Beck was owned by Fountains Abbey, whilst Bolton Priory had the eastern side of the dale. Only the base of the cross is the original stone – the shaft is a modern, and somewhat ugly, replacement.

A few yards from Nappa Gate is an iron trapdoor set in concrete. Below it an old shaft descends for some 75' to an extensive system of caverns and passages. These are the long-disused calamine mines. The presence of calamine was discovered here in the late 18th. century. It is an ore of zinc, which, after roasting, was used in the making of brass.

WARNING ———————————— DANGER
Take great care when crossing the limestone pavement above The Cove. Limestone, especially when wet, is slippery and treacherous, and a slip could result in a serious leg injury. This is a dangerous place for children, who should not be allowed to wander freely.

O.S. MAPS   Landranger Series (1:50 000) Sheet 98
(Wensleydale and Wharfedale)
Outdoor Leisure 10 (1:25 000) Yorkshire Dales
(Southern area)

© Jack Keighley 1990

38

CAVES & POTHOLES OF BIRKWITH

7 MILES

Set in the very heart of 'Three Peaks Country', the Birkwith area, a favourite haunt of cavers, abounds with interesting natural features. The walk takes us through pleasant limestone scenery to wild, rolling moorland, and follows the Pennine Way along two splendid old packhorse roads to visit a magnificent limestone gorge. Fine views and good conditions underfoot.

Browgill Cave

Leave Horton by the lane (no through road) between the Crown Hotel and the bridge. The tarmac ends at High Birkwith Farm. Here pay a small charge to continue up the private (and rough) track. Look out for another cart track turning up R, and park on grass at the junction.

Map ref: 804 772

①▸ Go up the branch cart track to a gate and stile, but before crossing the wall detour R to a stile into the ravine to see the cave. ②▸ On crossing the wall turn R off the cart track. Skirt the fence at the head of the ravine and maintain a level course (no path) with big limestone blocks on the L. ③▸ On approaching a small ravine with a wall running down it, bear R and drop down to a ladder-stile and footbridge (not seen until the last minute). Climb to the R of the slope opposite and continue alongside a wall on the R. (no path). There now follows over a mile of level walking on a wide limestone terrace (a clear path develops) to eventually reach a barn. ④▸ Cross the parallel broken walls at the barn and immediately turn L to a stile in the wall corner. Detour R along the broad Pennine Way through the gate to see Sell Gill Holes. ⑤▸ Return along the Pennine Way. ⑥▸ Detour R to see Cowskull Pot (there's a rowan sticking out of it) and, just beyond (about 100 yds from the track) the stream sink of Penyghent Long Churn. ⑦▸ Turn ½ L onto clear path (PW sign) over the hill and down to a ladder-stile by a shed. Follow the wall forward to reach a rough-metalled road. Turn L to Old Ing. ⑧▸ Turn R (PW sign). Follow the broad track for almost a mile. ⑨▸ Cross the packhorse bridge, turn sharp L, then curve R alongside the wall. ⑩▸ Turn L over a ladder-stile (FP Nether Lodge ⅞). Descend by the wall on the L to cross three waymarked fence stiles. Then over the hill and down to the farm. ⑪▸ Pass between the buildings (SP Birkwith and ladder-stile) Cross the footbridge and bear L (FP High Birkwith) up to a ladder-stile. ⑫▸ Turn R up a stony cart track (FP High Birkwith). Track becomes grassy before reaching a ladder-stile at God's Bridge, where a cave conveys a stream under the track. ⑬▸ Detour up alongside the wall to the R of the stream to see Browgill Cave, then return to the track and follow it to a ladder-stile. ⑭▸ Stay with the cart track and turn L up the road, or take a short cut over the hill.

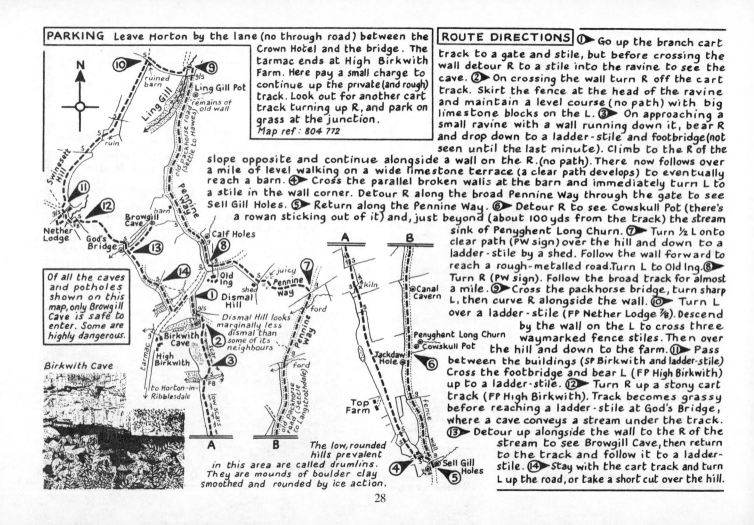

N

⑩ ⑨ ruined barn

Ling Gill Pot

remains of old wall

Ling Gill

old Packhorse road (Settle to Hawes)

ruin

Swinsett Hill

⑪

⑫

Browgill Cave

Nether Lodge

God's Bridge

⑬

⑭

Old Ing

Calf Holes

⑧

juicy

⑦

Pennine Way

shed

Dismal Hill

Dismal Hill looks marginally less dismal than some of its neighbours

Birkwith Cave

High Birkwith

to Horton-in-Ribblesdale

FB

low scars

old packhorse road (Settle to Langstrothdale)

ford

ford

Of all the caves and potholes shown on this map, only Browgill Cave is safe to enter. Some are highly dangerous.

Birkwith Cave

A   B

kiln

Canal Cavern

Penyghent Long Churn

Cowskull Pot

Jackdaw Hole

⑥

Top Farm

fence wall

Sell Gill Holes

④   ⑤

A   B

The low, rounded hills prevalent in this area are called drumlins. They are mounds of boulder clay smoothed and rounded by ice action.

THE CAVES AND POTHOLES BIRKWITH CAVE, at the head of a wooded ravine, is a low resurgence cave from which a sizeable stream emerges. SELL GILL HOLES has two entrances. The wet entrance is a stream sink above the Pennine Way track. Below the track is a dry entrance. Both lead to a huge cavern considered to be second in size only to the main chamber of Gaping Gill. JACKDAW HOLE is a huge, tree-fringed crater. COWSKULL POT occupies a rocky shakehole identified by its rowan tree. There are three entrances, one of which is a 70' shaft. PENYGHENT LONG CHURN lies just beyond and to the left of Cowskull (about 100 yds from the track). Here a small stream falls into a 100' shaft. Beware of slippery rock at the rim. CANAL CAVERN is a narrow rift at the trackside and leads to a 30' pitch into a stream. CALF HOLES, popular with cavers, is an impressive rocky stream sink. Don't get too near the edge — slippery rock. LING GILL POT is a small slot in a dry streambed 20 yds to the R. of the track. The sound of an underground waterfall can be heard. At GOD'S BRIDGE a 60' long through cave carries a stream under the track. BROWGILL CAVE is a magnificent resurgence cave. The issuing stream is that which disappears at Calf Holes.

Ling Gill Bridge

Ling Gill is a deeply-cut and wooded limestone ravine. It is a nature reserve, and within its precipitous confines is preserved much of the natural vegetation of the limestone fells. The sturdy old gritstone packhorse bridge at its head has an inscribed tablet (now scarcely decipherable) informing us that the bridge was repaired in 1765 at the charge of the whole West Rideing'.

O.S. MAPS   Landranger Series (1 : 50 000) Sheet 98
(Wensleydale and Wharfedale)
© Jack Keighley 1990 . Outdoor Leisure 2 (1 : 25 000) Y.D. Western area

---

WALKS IN THE YORKSHIRE DALES

39

THE ASCENT OF GREAT HAW

(FROM WEST SCRAFTON)

6 MILES

A Jekyll and Hyde of a walk. On a dull, wet day it will seem dreary and depressing — an eminently forgettable experience. Do it in late summer sunshine, when the moor is a sea of purple and there is a riot of colour where all was once drab. On such a day it will uplift the soul.

JKeighley

Bridge Cottage,
West Scrafton

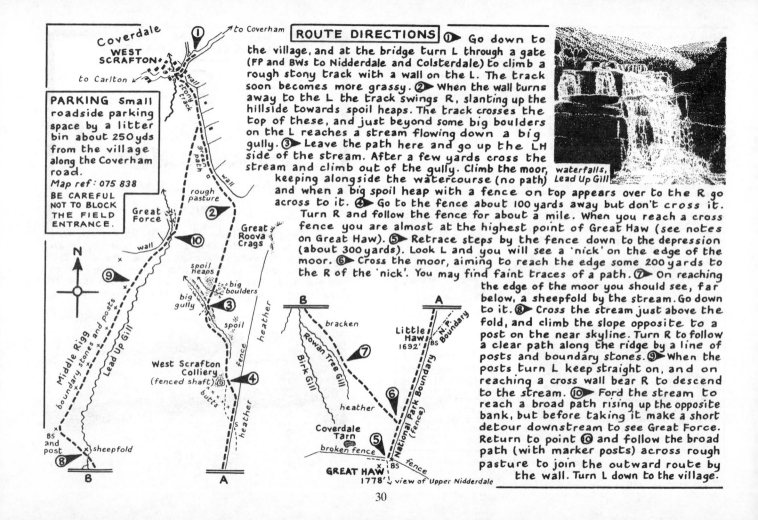

ROUTE DIRECTIONS

① Go down to the village, and at the bridge turn L through a gate (FP and BWs to Nidderdale and Colsterdale) to climb a rough stony track with a wall on the L. The track soon becomes more grassy. ② When the wall turns away to the L the track swings R, slanting up the hillside towards spoil heaps. The track crosses the top of these, and just beyond some big boulders on the L reaches a stream flowing down a big gully. ③ Leave the path here and go up the LH side of the stream. After a few yards cross the stream and climb out of the gully. Climb the moor, keeping alongside the watercourse (no path) and when a big spoil heap with a fence on top appears over to the R go across to it. ④ Go to the fence about 100 yards away but don't cross it. Turn R and follow the fence for about a mile. When you reach a cross fence you are almost at the highest point of Great Haw (see notes on Great Haw). ⑤ Retrace steps by the fence down to the depression (about 300 yards). Look L and you will see a 'nick' on the edge of the moor. ⑥ Cross the moor, aiming to reach the edge some 200 yards to the R of the 'nick'. You may find faint traces of a path. ⑦ On reaching the edge of the moor you should see, far below, a sheepfold by the stream. Go down to it. ⑧ Cross the stream just above the fold, and climb the slope opposite to a post on the near skyline. Turn R to follow a clear path along the ridge by a line of posts and boundary stones. ⑨ When the posts turn L keep straight on, and on reaching a cross wall bear R to descend to the stream. ⑩ Ford the stream to reach a broad path rising up the opposite bank, but before taking it make a short detour downstream to see Great Force. Return to point ⑩ and follow the broad path (with marker posts) across rough pasture to join the outward route by the wall. Turn L down to the village.

waterfalls, Lead Up Gill

Coverdale
WEST SCRAFTON
to Coverham
to Carlton

PARKING Small roadside parking space by a litter bin about 250 yds from the village along the Coverham road.
Map ref: 075 838
BE CAREFUL NOT TO BLOCK THE FIELD ENTRANCE.

rough pasture
Great Force
Great Roova Crags
spoil heaps
big boulders
big gully
spoil
West Scrafton Colliery (fenced shaft)
butts
heather
fence
Middle Rigg
boundary stones and posts
Lead Up Gill
BS and post
sheepfold
B

bracken
Rowan Tree Gill
Birk Gill
heather
Coverdale Tarn
broken fence
Little Haw 1692'
N.P. Boundary
BS
National Park Boundary (fence)
fence
GREAT HAW 1778' view of Upper Nidderdale

30

GREAT HAW is almost the highest point of the lonely moors which separate Coverdale from Colsterdale to the east and Nidderdale to the south. Its summit is, to say the least, undistinguished — a featureless, soggy lump — but it is a good viewpoint for Upper Nidderdale. From the fence corner at point ⑤ keep on straight ahead (beware of hidden bogholes) for about 100 yards for the view down Nidderdale to Gouthwaite Reservoir. A similar detour westward from the fence corner will bring Coverdale Tarn into view.

COAL MINING

old shaft, West Scrafton Colliery

Coal seams occur quite frequently in the Yoredale series of rocks around Wensleydale, though the coal is not of top quality. The first spoil heaps met on the walk mark a place where a seam close to the surface was mined from levels. The shaft on the moor top (West Scrafton Colliery) was in use until early this century, and much of the coal it produced was used for lime burning and lead smelting. The rim of the flooded shaft is loose and crumbly, so keep away from the edge.

Serene and peaceful COVERDALE is the longest of Wensleydale's many side-valleys. 'Cover' — pronounced to rhyme with 'hover' — is an ancient British word meaning 'the stream in the deep ravine'. The houses of WEST SCRAFTON are closely grouped around a tiny green. The large house near the telephone box was once the Moorhen Inn. 'Scrafton' is Saxon for 'the town by the hollow'.

O.S. MAPS :   Landranger Series (1:50 000) Sheet 99
(Northallerton and Ripon)
Outdoor Leisure 30 (1:25 000) Yorkshire Dales
(Northern and Central areas)

© Jack Keighley 1990

LOWER GARSDALE

6 MILES

Rights-of-way in Garsdale are few and far between, and this gentle valley stroll is one of the very few walks available in what is probably the least-known dale in the National Park. Other than below Danny Bridge, where the Clough River plunges through a fine limestone gorge, the scenery is peaceful rather than exciting.

Danny Bridge   JKeighley

PARKING Large car park (with information board) by the A684 Sedbergh to Hawes road about 2¼ miles from Sedbergh at Longstone Common.
Map ref: 695 913

ROUTE DIRECTIONS ① Walk down the tarmac lane (SP Sedgwick Trail), cross Danny Bridge and continue along the lane for a further 1¼ miles. ② Go through a gate on the L with a sign 'Bellow Hill' (FP Pike Hill ¼) and follow the cart track. On coming to a gate don't go through it, but go forward along the RH side of a wall to a stile. Continue by the wall, but on approaching the end of the next field bear R down to a stile. Go straight across the next field aiming towards the farmhouse, in front of which is a stile leading onto a farm lane. ③ Turn R down the farm lane and L along the main road. ④ About 100 yds after passing Birkrigg Farm on the R take a stile on the L (FP's Hill ¾ or Dales View). Follow the wall on the L, then turn L to go up the farm road. Keep on past the farm, staying between walls. ⑤ Turn R to pass in front of a barn through two gates, then go straight across three fields, using stiles, to reach the next farm. ⑥ Pass very close to the front of the farmhouse to a stile in the wall. Cross the next field towards another farm, but just before reaching it go down to a gate on the R. ⑦ Go down the farm road for a few yards before turning L through a gap in the wall. Cross the field, keeping roughly parallel with the wall on the L, to a stile, and continue across the next field to a gate. Turn R towards the house and pass through two gates immediately to the L of it to reach a green path going down through trees. ⑧ Turn R along the main road, and in about 100 yds turn L through a stile (FP New Bridge). Go straight across the field to a gate, then follow the riverside path. ⑨ At a point where a low concrete bridge crosses the river (but we don't), the path passes along a narrow space between the river bank and a wall. ⑩ At New Bridge cross the main road and go down some steps to resume the riverside walk, but on reaching the next field boundary don't cross the stile. Turn R and go up alongside the fence. ⑪ Use gates to pass round to the L of a barn, then turn L and follow a line of stiles to reach a gate just below a farm. ⑫ Keep L of the farm, then bear R to a stile in the field corner. Go up to a gate to the R of a barn, then turn L behind the barn and go forward to reach a farm road leading onto the lane back to Danny Bridge. On crossing the bridge turn R along the river bank (see notes on the Sedgwick Geological Trail).

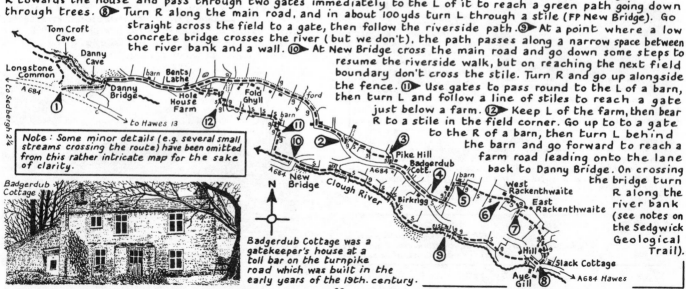

Note: Some minor details (e.g. several small streams crossing the route) have been omitted from this rather intricate map for the sake of clarity.

Badgerdub Cottage was a gatekeeper's house at a toll bar on the turnpike road which was built in the early years of the 19th. century.

32

THE SEDGWICK GEOLOGICAL TRAIL is named after the pioneer geologist Adam Sedgwick (1785-1873), whose father was Vicar of Dent. The trail follows the south bank of the river downstream from Danny Bridge, along the line of the Dent Fault. There are 12 numbered location posts and a detailed leaflet, which is on sale at any of the National Park Centres. Visitors without a leaflet, who are just admiring the scenery, need go no further than post 8 — from there turning back along a path slanting up the moor.

● The fells flanking the dale are Baugh Fell to the north and Rise Hill to the south.

● East Rackenthwaite stands on the site of a grange of Coverham Abbey.

● Danny Cave is a small resurgence in the south bank of the river a few yards below the bridge.

● Tom Croft Cave is near location post Nº 7. The large entrance soon closes to a small hole.

● This is essentially a dry weather walk. After rain the field sections can be very muddy.

● Many of the gates on this walk are in a poor state of repair, and some will be found to be difficult, or impossible, to open.

O.S. MAPS : Landranger Series (1:50 000) Sheet 98
(Wensleydale and Wharfedale)
Outdoor Leisure 2 (1:25 000) Yorkshire Dales
(Western area)

© Jack Keighley 1990

41

LEYBURN SHAWL

6 MILES

Running west from Leyburn is The Shawl, an elevated limestone terrace along which a delectable path winds through beautiful woodland and gives glorious views of mid-Wensleydale. The low-level return route passes through the fine parkland of Bolton Hall to Wensley, with its quite outstanding parish church — one of the loveliest in the Dales.

path on The Shawl J Keighley

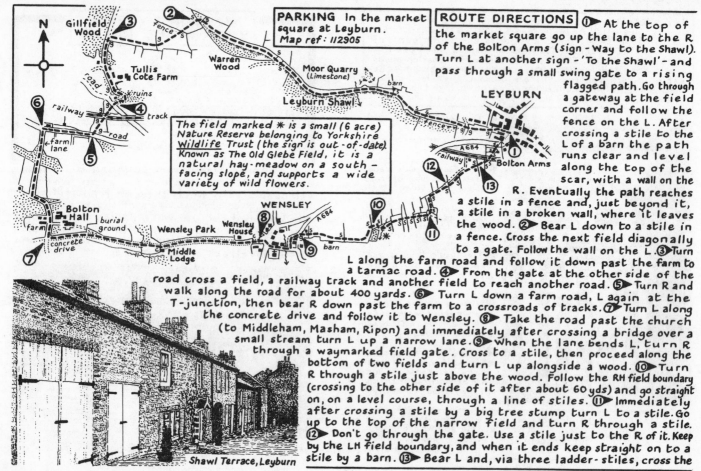

PARKING In the market square at Leyburn. Map ref: 112905

The field marked ✳ is a small (6 acre) Nature Reserve belonging to Yorkshire Wildlife Trust (the sign is out-of-date). Known as The Old Glebe Field, it is a natural hay-meadow on a south-facing slope, and supports a wide variety of wild flowers.

Map labels: N, Gillfield Wood, Tullis Cote Farm, Warren Wood, Moor Quarry (Limestone), barn, Leyburn Shawl, railway, road, ruins, track, farm lane, LEYBURN, A684, railway, Bolton Arms, Bolton Hall, burial ground, farm, concrete drive, Wensley Park, Middle Lodge, Wensley House, WENSLEY, A684, barn

ROUTE DIRECTIONS ① At the top of the market square go up the lane to the R of the Bolton Arms (sign - Way to the Shawl). Turn L at another sign - 'To the Shawl' - and pass through a small swing gate to a rising flagged path. Go through a gateway at the field corner and follow the fence on the L. After crossing a stile to the L of a barn the path runs clear and level along the top of the scar, with a wall on the R. Eventually the path reaches a stile in a fence and, just beyond it, a stile in a broken wall, where it leaves the wood. ② Bear L down to a stile in a fence. Cross the next field diagonally to a gate. Follow the wall on the L. ③ Turn L along the farm road and follow it down past the farm to a tarmac road. ④ From the gate at the other side of the road cross a field, a railway track and another field to reach another road. ⑤ Turn R and walk along the road for about 400 yards. ⑥ Turn L down a farm road, L again at the T-junction, then bear R down past the farm to a crossroads of tracks. ⑦ Turn L along the concrete drive and follow it to Wensley. ⑧ Take the road past the church (to Middleham, Masham, Ripon) and immediately after crossing a bridge over a small stream turn L up a narrow lane. ⑨ When the lane bends L, turn R through a waymarked field gate. Cross to a stile, then proceed along the bottom of two fields and turn L up alongside a wood. ⑩ Turn R through a stile just above the wood. Follow the RH field boundary (crossing to the other side of it after about 60 yds) and go straight on, on a level course, through a line of stiles. ⑪ Immediately after crossing a stile by a big tree stump turn L to a stile. Go up to the top of the narrow field and turn R through a stile. ⑫ Don't go through the gate. Use a stile just to the R of it. Keep by the LH field boundary, and when it ends keep straight on to a stile by a barn. ⑬ Bear L and, via three ladder-stiles, cross the

Shawl Terrace, Leyburn

34

railway (with due care, for it is in use here, serving the quarry). Go up through a stile to two gates onto the main road on the outskirts of Leyburn.

LEGEND HAS IT THAT LEYBURN SHAWL IS SO CALLED BECAUSE MARY QUEEN OF SCOTS DROPPED HER SHAWL HERE IN ATTEMPTING TO ESCAPE FROM BOLTON CASTLE, WHERE SHE WAS HELD PRISONER IN 1568. IT IS MORE LIKELY, THOUGH LESS ROMANTIC, THAT THE UNUSUAL NAME IS DERIVED FROM *SCHALLS*, A CORRUPTION OF THE SCANDINAVIAN *SKALI*, MEANING 'HUTS'.

BOLTON HALL was built in 1678 by the Marquis of Winchester, who married the daughter of the last Lord Scrope. It was rebuilt in 1902 after being extensively damaged by fire.
The house contains many fine paintings - notably some by Van Dyck.

In the 13th. century WENSLEY was the only market town in Wensleydale. Disaster struck in 1563, when the population was decimated by the plague. Wensley never recovered, and its market moved to Leyburn. The Parish Church(Holy Trinity) dates from 1245, the aisles being rebuilt c 1330 and the tower in 1719. Of special interest are the fine memorial brass on the Sanctuary floor, the choir stalls (1527), the pulpit (1760), the font (1662) which has some upside-down letters in its inscription and the large box pews of the Bolton family. The wooden screen behind these pews and the large wooden box near the door are from Easby Abbey.

O.S. MAPS :   *Landranger Series (1 : 50 000) Sheet 99
                    (Northallerton and Ripon)
              Outdoor Leisure 30 (1 : 25 000) Yorkshire Dales
                    (Northern and Central areas)*

© Jack Keighley 1990

BURNSALL, THORPE & LINTON

5½ MILES

An easy walk, but allow plenty of time, for there is much to admire and linger over. Two contrasting villages are visited — sleepy Thorpe, hidden away between reef knolls, and the lovely Linton, famed for its 'picture-postcard' beauty. From the ancient church the return to Burnsall must surely rank as the most beautiful riverside walk in the Dales.

Linton   *J Keighley*

PARKING Car park and toilets just below Burnsall Bridge, or large field car park (not always open) with access from Appletreewick road.
Map ref : 033 612

ROUTE DIRECTIONS ① Leave Burnsall by the Grassington road from the Red Lion Inn. ② At the first bend go through a gate on the L (FP Thorpe 1½) into a little yard. Go through another gate to a stile in the wall behind it. The path runs from stile to stile in a straight line across a number of narrow fields. ③ Bear R up to a concealed stile, which lies just beyond the wall corner, level with the trees. Proceed along the centre of the next field and cross a narrow lane (FP Thorpe) to continue alongside a wall for about 50 yds. ④ Bear L away from wall (FP sign). Pass to the R of a pair of ash trees, then aim towards the LH end of a wood seen ahead. ⑤ Pass round the back of the wood and up through a gate to a ladder-stile. Turn L along the lane and follow it to Thorpe. ⑥ Leave Thorpe by the road going uphill from the letterbox, and turn L when the road forks. ⑦ Turn R through a stile near a ruin (FP Linton). Go down past the end of a wood to a ladder-stile. Keep straight on to a cart track and follow it down to emerge between buildings onto a tarmac lane. ⑧ Turn R into the village. ⑨ At the far end of the village turn R along the main road, and after a few yards fork R up a lane. ⑩ Join the main road for about 80 yds before taking a stile on the L (FP Linton Church and Falls). The path leads down to the tarmac lane to Linton Church. Cross a stile at the far end of the churchyard and go straight forward to the stepping-stones. ALTERNATIVE ROUTE - If the river is high the stepping-stones may be impassable. If so, return along the lane from the church and at the last house on the R (Falls House) turn sharp right down a lane (Public Footpath Grassington). The lane leads to a tiny bridge, but don't cross it. Go along the path behind the houses to the big footbridge, and immediately after crossing it take a stile on the R (FP Hebden). Walk parallel to the river to reach a lane. Turn R to a stile at the end of the lane, and cross it to reach the path from the stepping-stones at ⑪ Head

N

Linton Falls
FB
barn
fish farm
car park and toilets
Linton Church
stepping stones
FB
⑪
⑨
B6160
Inn
YHA
⑩
LINTON
⑧
view of Gt. Whernside directly in line with Grassington
BW to B6160
cart track
ruin
Cracoe Monument seen on skyline
⑦
Give way to oncoming traffic on the remarkable suspension bridge, built in 1885 by a local blacksmith. Nearby are some obsolete stepping-stones.
Dales Way
River Wharfe
suspension bridge
⑫
postman's steps
Loup Scar
ELBOLTON HILL
THORPE
⑥
⑤
KAIL HILL
2 ash trees
lane
④
③
PLEASE WALK IN SINGLE FILE ACROSS THE MEADOWS
②
①
BURNSALL
car park and toilets

Elbolton Hill and Kail Hill are 'reef knolls' - low rounded hills composed of a particularly pure form of limestone. There are several of these along the line of the North Craven Fault south of Grassington, their light-green colour contrasting sharply with the dark gritstone moorland. One of them is being eaten into by the monstrous Swinden Quarry, seen (unfortunately) from near Linton.

slightly R across the field, over a tiny footbridge, to reach a gate and the clear riverside path. ⑫► Cross the suspension bridge and continue downstream on a 'made' path. Stay close to the river all the way back to Burnsall.

Thorpe

Thorpe, lying in a hollow between knolls of limestone, is often referred to as 'the hidden village', and it is said that people found refuge here from Scottish raiders in the Middle Ages. In the 19th century the village had a thriving boot- and shoe-making industry. The Georgian manor-house was gutted by fire in 1939, but has since been repaired. Linton, one of Yorkshire's prettiest villages, has cottages of every period. The much-photographed green has a little beck which is crossed by three bridges - clapper, packhorse and modern road. The elaborate Fountaine's Hospital dominates the village. It was built by Richard Fountaine as almshouses in 1721.

❀ THE PARISH CHURCH OF ST. MICHAEL AND ALL ❀ ANGELS is, despite its somewhat squat and uninspiring external appearance, a place of great beauty and interest. Although largely rebuilt in the 15th. century the church dates back to about 1150. The oldest parts of the structure are the two arches in the north aisle, and the font is a relic of the original Norman church. Kirk Yetts (Church Gates), ❀ the house which stands by the churchyard ❀ gate, was formerly an inn.

O.S. MAPS : Landranger Series (1 : 50 000) Sheet 98
(Wensleydale and Wharfedale)
Outdoor Leisure 10 (1 : 25 000) Yorkshire Dales
(Southern area)

© Jack Keighley 1990

WHITE SCAR CAVE & MEREGILL HOLE

6¼ MILES

An exploration, both on and below the surface, of a vast limestone plateau on the western flanks of Ingleborough. This is an exceptionally interesting walk, with visits to a famous show cave and an awesome pothole. The gleaming limestone pavements and the tremendous tiered ramparts of Raven Scar provide scenery of immense grandeur.

Ingleborough from Fell Lane

J Keighley

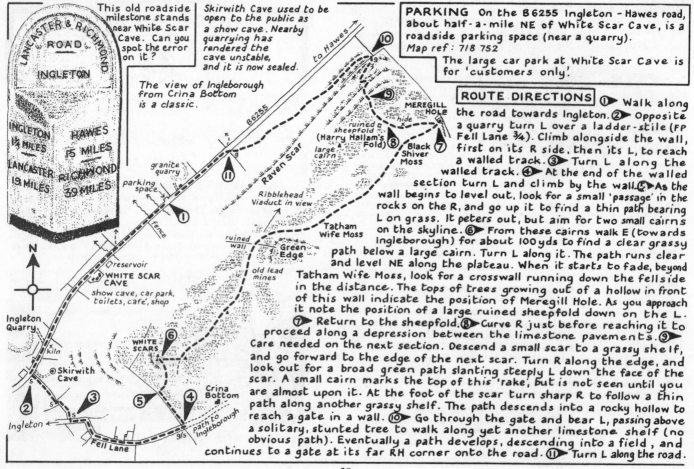

This old roadside milestone stands near White Scar Cave. Can you spot the error on it?

LANCASTER & RICHMOND ROAD
INGLETON
INGLETON 1¼ MILES   HAWES 15 MILES
LANCASTER 19 MILES   RICHMOND 39 MILES

Skirwith Cave used to be open to the public as a show cave. Nearby quarrying has rendered the cave unstable, and it is now sealed.

The view of Ingleborough from Crina Bottom is a classic.

PARKING On the B6255 Ingleton - Hawes road, about half-a-mile NE of White Scar Cave, is a roadside parking space (near a quarry).
Map ref: 718 752
The large car park at White Scar Cave is for 'customers only'.

ROUTE DIRECTIONS ① Walk along the road towards Ingleton. ② Opposite a quarry turn L over a ladder-stile (FP Fell Lane ¾). Climb alongside the wall, first on its R side, then its L, to reach a walled track. ③ Turn L along the walled track. ④ At the end of the walled section turn L and climb by the wall. ⑤ As the wall begins to level out, look for a small 'passage' in the rocks on the R, and go up it to find a thin path bearing L on grass. It peters out, but aim for two small cairns on the skyline. ⑥ From these cairns walk E (towards Ingleborough) for about 100 yds to find a clear grassy path below a large cairn. Turn L along it. The path runs clear and level NE along the plateau. When it starts to fade, beyond Tatham Wife Moss, look for a crosswall running down the fellside in the distance. The tops of trees growing out of a hollow in front of this wall indicate the position of Meregill Hole. As you approach it note the position of a large ruined sheepfold down on the L. ⑦ Return to the sheepfold. ⑧ Curve R just before reaching it to proceed along a depression between the limestone pavements. ⑨ Care needed on the next section. Descend a small scar to a grassy shelf, and go forward to the edge of the next scar. Turn R along the edge, and look out for a broad green path slanting steeply L down the face of the scar. A small cairn marks the top of this 'rake', but is not seen until you are almost upon it. At the foot of the scar turn sharp R to follow a thin path along another grassy shelf. The path descends into a rocky hollow to reach a gate in a wall. ⑩ Go through the gate and bear L, passing above a solitary, stunted tree to walk along yet another limestone shelf (no obvious path). Eventually a path develops, descending into a field, and continues to a gate at its far RH corner onto the road. ⑪ Turn L along the road.

to Hawes
B6255
granite quarry
parking space
Raven Scar
Ribblehead Viaduct in view
ruined wall
old lead mines
Tatham Wife Moss
Green Edge
Crina Bottom
path to Ingleborough
N
reservoir
WHITE SCAR CAVE
show cave, car park, toilets, café, shop
Ingleton Quarry
kiln
Skirwith Cave
WHITE SCARS
fence
Ingleton
Fell Lane
MEREGILL HOLE
hide
ruined sheepfold (Harry Hallam's Fold)
large cairn
Black Shiver Moss

38

WHITE SCAR CAVE

White Scar Cave was discovered in 1923 by C.F.C. Long, a Cambridge undergraduate. The original entrance was a very low passage, negociable only by flat-out crawling. Very soon after discovery an artificial entrance tunnel was blasted in order to open up the cave to the public. Visitors may now penetrate half-a-mile into the hillside along a fine stream passage well-decorated with stalagmites and stalactites, many of them 'alive' with dripping water, and attractive flowstone formations many thousands of years old. The show cave ends at a barrier, but beyond this the cave system extends for several miles. Special guided Adventure Trips can be arranged for groups who wish to explore beyond the barrier. The show cave is open daily throughout the year.

C.F.C. Long tableau, White Scar Cave

> MEREGILL HOLE is one of the district's major potholes. It is a long rift with walls dropping vertically for some 40-50 feet into a deep lake (the Mere, from which the pothole gets its name.) The stream which plunges into the hole can be diverted in order to reduce the depth of the Mere and thus simplify (!!) the potholer's descent into the lower shafts and passages. These initially head straight back into the hillside, the stream descending to a depth of over 400 feet before reaching a bedding plane and flowing away towards the valley.

The route is not an official right-of-way between points ④ and ⑪, but it is open country, much-frequented by potholers, and there should be no objection.

THE WALK IS NOT RECOMMENDED IN MIST OR SNOW

O.S. MAPS : Landranger Series (1:50 000) Sheet 98
(Wensleydale and Wharfedale)
Outdoor Leisure 2 (1:25 000) Yorkshire Dales
(western area)

© Jack Keighley 1990

BOLTON ABBEY & HAZLEWOOD MOOR

6¼ MILES

Bolton Abbey is a renowned beauty spot — possibly the best-known and best-loved place in the whole of the Dales. This walk takes us from the breathtaking beauty of the riverside scenery to the wild landscapes of the moorland to the east. Before starting check that the Access Area is open — and don't take the dog.

Bolton Hall   JKeighley

39

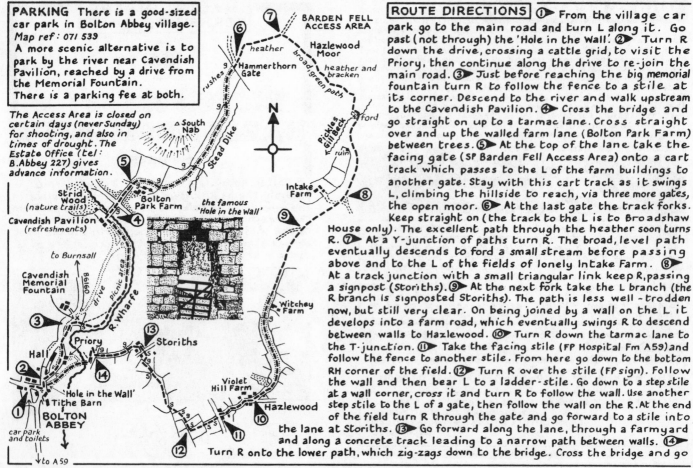

PARKING There is a good-sized car park in Bolton Abbey village. Map ref: 071 539
A more scenic alternative is to park by the river near Cavendish Pavilion, reached by a drive from the Memorial Fountain.
There is a parking fee at both.

The Access Area is closed on certain days (never Sunday) for shooting, and also in times of drought. The Estate Office (tel: B.Abbey 227) gives advance information.

ROUTE DIRECTIONS

① From the village car park go to the main road and turn L along it. Go past (not through) the 'Hole in the Wall'. ② Turn R down the drive, crossing a cattle grid, to visit the Priory, then continue along the drive to re-join the main road. ③ Just before reaching the big memorial fountain turn R to follow the fence to a stile at its corner. Descend to the river and walk upstream to the Cavendish Pavilion. ④ Cross the bridge and go straight on up to a tarmac lane. Cross straight over and up the walled farm lane (Bolton Park Farm) between trees. ⑤ At the top of the lane take the facing gate (SP Barden Fell Access Area) onto a cart track which passes to the L of the farm buildings to another gate. Stay with this cart track as it swings L, climbing the hillside to reach, via three more gates, the open moor. ⑥ At the last gate the track forks. Keep straight on (the track to the L is to Broadshaw House only). The excellent path through the heather soon turns R. ⑦ At a Y-junction of paths turn R. The broad, level path eventually descends to ford a small stream before passing above and to L of the fields of lonely Intake Farm. ⑧ At a track junction with a small triangular link keep R, passing a signpost (Storiths). ⑨ At the next fork take the L branch (the R branch is signposted Storiths). The path is less well-trodden now, but still very clear. On being joined by a wall on the L it develops into a farm road, which eventually swings R to descend between walls to Hazlewood. ⑩ Turn R down the tarmac lane to the T-junction. ⑪ Take the facing stile (FP Hospital Fm A59) and follow the fence to another stile. From here go down to the bottom RH corner of the field. ⑫ Turn R over the stile (FP sign). Follow the wall and then bear L to a ladder-stile. Go down to a step stile at a wall corner, cross it and turn R to follow the wall. Use another step stile to the L of a gate, then follow the wall on the R. At the end of the field turn R through the gate and go forward to a stile into the lane at Storiths. ⑬ Go forward along the lane, through a farmyard and along a concrete track leading to a narrow path between walls. ⑭ Turn R onto the lower path, which zig-zags down to the bridge. Cross the bridge and go

40

straight forward up the wide path to the 'Hole in the Wall'.

BOLTON *ABBEY* is the name of the village. The monastic ruin is properly called BOLTON *PRIORY*, and was established in 1154 by Augustinians who moved here from Embsay. The nave, having been walled off from the rest of the church by Richard Moone, Bolton's last prior, before the Dissolution, remains in use as a most beautiful Priory Church. Because of the Dissolution the fine West Tower, begun in 1520, was never completed. BOLTON HALL was originally the Priory's gatehouse. The Priory, in its heyday, owned much land and property in Wharfedale, Littondale, Airedale and Malhamdale. The huge TITHE BARN, in the village behind the Post Office, is built on the site of the original medieval building.

the Tithe Barn

The CAVENDISH MEMORIAL is a large, ornate fountain erected in 1886 in memory of Lord Frederick Cavendish, a local Liberal M.P. who was assassinated in Phoenix Park, Dublin, in May 1882.

The CAVENDISH PAVILION was built in Edwardian times as a shooting-lodge.

The walk passes through this farmyard at Storiths

This is a fine walk in all conditions except deep snow, when the tracks on the moor may be obliterated.

O.S. MAPS :   Landranger Series (1 : 50 000) Sheet 104
                              (Leeds, Bradford and Harrogate)
              Outdoor Leisure 10 (1 : 25 000) Yorkshire Dales
                                      (Southern area)

© Jack Keighley 1990

CASTLE BOLTON & CARPERBY

8¼ MILES

A bracing walk along the lower slopes of the limestone hills forming Wensleydale's northern flank. The gradients are gentle, and the outstanding feature of the walk is the beautiful and panoramic view across the broad and verdant dale. Do it on a warm day in high summer, when the air is sweet with the fragrance of flowers and new-mown hay.

Bolton Castle   JKeighley

41

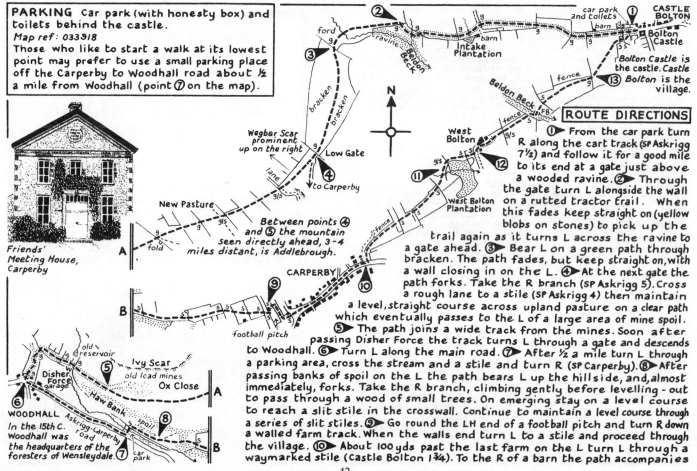

PARKING Car park (with honesty box) and toilets behind the castle.
Map ref: 033918
Those who like to start a walk at its lowest point may prefer to use a small parking place off the Carperby to Woodhall road about ½ a mile from Woodhall (point ⑦ on the map).

Friends' Meeting House, Carperby

WOODHALL
In the 15th C. Woodhall was the headquarters of the foresters of Wensleydale.

ford
ravine
Beldon Beck
Intake Plantation
barn

CASTLE BOLTON
car park and toilets
barn
Bolton Castle

Bolton Castle is the castle. Castle Bolton is the village.

fence
Beldon Beck
F.B.
fence

West Bolton
West Bolton Plantation

Wegber Scar prominent up on the right
Low Gate
to Carperby

New Pasture
fold

Between points ④ and ⑤ the mountain seen directly ahead, 3-4 miles distant, is Addlebrough.

CARPERBY

football pitch

old reservoir
Ivy Scar
old lead mines
Ox Close

Disher Force
garage
Haw Bank
spoil
Askrigg-Carperby road
car park

ROUTE DIRECTIONS

① From the car park turn R along the cart track (SP Askrigg 7½) and follow it for a good mile to its end at a gate just above a wooded ravine. ② Through the gate turn L alongside the wall on a rutted tractor trail. When this fades keep straight on (yellow blobs on stones) to pick up the trail again as it turns L across the ravine to a gate ahead. ③ Bear L on a green path through bracken. The path fades, but keep straight on, with a wall closing in on the L. ④ At the next gate the path forks. Take the R branch (SP Askrigg 5). Cross a rough lane to a stile (SP Askrigg 4) then maintain a level, straight course across upland pasture on a clear path which eventually passes to the L of a large area of mine spoil. ⑤ The path joins a wide track from the mines. Soon after passing Disher Force the track turns L through a gate and descends to Woodhall. ⑥ Turn L along the main road. ⑦ After ½ a mile turn L through a parking area, cross the stream and a stile and turn R (SP Carperby). ⑧ After passing banks of spoil on the L the path bears L up the hillside, and, almost immediately, forks. Take the R branch, climbing gently before levelling-out to pass through a wood of small trees. On emerging stay on a level course to reach a slit stile in the crosswall. Continue to maintain a level course through a series of slit stiles. ⑨ Go round the LH end of a football pitch and turn R down a walled farm track. When the walls end turn L to a stile and proceed through the village. ⑩ About 100 yds past the last farm on the L turn L through a waymarked stile (Castle Bolton 1¾). To the R of a barn the path accompanies

42

a cart track uphill (at the time of writing an electric fence separated the two). When the cart track turns L keep straight on, making a beeline for the castle now seen in the distance. The route soon becomes clear and very well waymarked. ⑪▶ Skirt round the LH side of the wood and head for the farm. ⑫▶ Pass to the immediate R of the farm and continue forward with a fence on the L. ⑬▶ From the metal field gate bear L, aiming for the trees to the L of the castle. Turn R at a signpost (FP Castle Bolton) to pass through two final slit stiles.

> The imposing BOLTON CASTLE was erected by Richard, the first Lord Scrope, as a fortified manor house rather than a castle, and it took 18 years to build (starting in 1379). Mary Queen of Scots was imprisoned here (in some comfort) from July 1568 to January 1569. During the Civil War the castle – a Royalist garrison – was besieged by the Roundheads, and surrendered in 1645. The castle contains a folk museum and restaurant, and is open daily March to October (10 a.m. to 5 p.m.).

CASTLE BOLTON is a pleasant village with a spacious green lined by cottages which once were lead-miners' homes. The tiny, well-kept church of St. Oswald lies literally in the shadow of the castle – so much so that the sundial near the porch was rendered obsolete when the castle was built. The church pre-dates the castle by over 50 years, and is unusual in that there is no structural division between the chancel and the nave, which are equal in width. CARPERBY has a large

market cross
Carperby

market cross dated 1674. The village was granted its market charter in 1305, and was originally a grange of Easby Abbey. In the 17th. century Carperby became a centre of Quakerism, and its largest building is the Friends' Meeting House (1864).

> O.S. MAPS : Landranger Series (1:50 000) Sheet 98
> (Wensleydale and Wharfedale)
> Outdoor Leisure 30 (1:25 000) Yorkshire Dales
> (Northern and Central areas)

㊺

COLSTERDALE

6¼ MILES

Beautiful Colsterdale, remote and secluded, is one of the least known and, consequently, most peaceful dales. On a sunny day, when the heather is in bloom, or later, when the autumn colours glow, this is an absolute gem of a walk. There is a rich variety of scenery and a succession of splendid vantage points.

Slipstone Crags   JKeighley

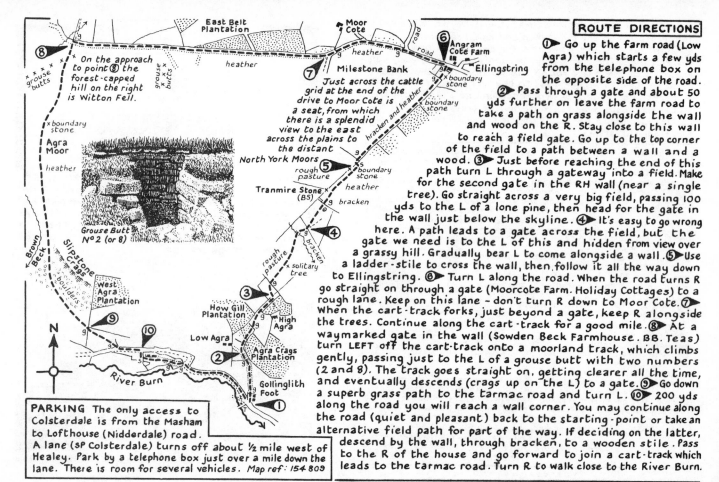

East Belt Plantation

Moor Cote

6 Angram Cote Farm

Ellingstring

7 Milestone Bank

Just across the cattle grid at the end of the drive to Moor Cote is a seat, from which there is a splendid view to the east across the plains to the distant North York Moors

8

On the approach to point 8 the forest-capped hill on the right is Witton Fell.

grouse butts

grouse butts

x boundary stone

x boundary stone

x boundary stone

Agra Moor

heather

heather

bracken and heather

5

rough pasture

x boundary stone

heather

Tranmire Stone (B5)

bracken

4

bracken

rough pasture

solitary tree

Grouse Butt Nº 2 (or 8)

Brown Beck

Slipstone Crags

boulders

West Agra Plantation

9

3

How Gill Plantation

High Agra

Low Agra

2

Agra Crags Plantation

10

N

River Burn

Gollinglith Foot

1

PARKING The only access to Colsterdale is from the Masham to Lofthouse (Nidderdale) road. A lane (SP Colsterdale) turns off about ½ mile west of Healey. Park by a telephone box just over a mile down the lane. There is room for several vehicles. Map ref: 154 809

① Go up the farm road (Low Agra) which starts a few yds from the telephone box on the opposite side of the road. ② Pass through a gate and about 50 yds further on leave the farm road to take a path on grass alongside the wall and wood on the R. Stay close to this wall to reach a field gate. Go up to the top corner of the field to a path between a wall and a wood. ③ Just before reaching the end of this path turn L through a gateway into a field. Make for the second gate in the RH wall (near a single tree). Go straight across a very big field, passing 100 yds to the L of a lone pine, then head for the gate in the wall just below the skyline. ④ It's easy to go wrong here. A path leads to a gate across the field, but the gate we need is to the L of this and hidden from view over a grassy hill. Gradually bear L to come alongside a wall. ⑤ Use a ladder-stile to cross the wall, then follow it all the way down to Ellingstring. ⑥ Turn L along the road. When the road turns R go straight on through a gate (Moorcote Farm. Holiday Cottages) to a rough lane. Keep on this lane — don't turn R down to Moor Cote. ⑦ When the cart-track forks, just beyond a gate, keep R alongside the trees. Continue along the cart-track for a good mile. ⑧ At a waymarked gate in the wall (Sowden Beck Farmhouse. BB. Teas) turn LEFT off the cart-track onto a moorland track, which climbs gently, passing just to the L of a grouse butt with two numbers (2 and 8). The track goes straight on, getting clearer all the time, and eventually descends (crags up on the L) to a gate. ⑨ Go down a superb grass path to the tarmac road and turn L. ⑩ 200 yds along the road you will reach a wall corner. You may continue along the road (quiet and pleasant) back to the starting-point or take an alternative field path for part of the way. If deciding on the latter, descend by the wall, through bracken, to a wooden stile. Pass to the R of the house and go forward to join a cart-track which leads to the tarmac road. Turn R to walk close to the River Burn.

THREE OF THE BOUNDARY STONES SEEN ON THE WALK

Tranmire Stone   *near point ⑤*   *on Agra Moor*

COLSTERDALE is quiet now, but has seen its share of bustle and activity, for it was once a coalfield (a 'colster' was a medieval coal merchant). In the Middle Ages coal and lead mines in the valley belonged to Jervaulx Abbey. The track along the south side of the dale is still known as the Coal Road. At the beginning of this century Leeds Corporation planned to flood Colsterdale, but fortunately the scheme was abandoned and Leighton reservoir was built instead. During the First World War the 15th Battalion, the West Yorkshire Regiment - the famous 'Leeds Pals' - had a training camp at Breary Banks, south of the river. The Battalion was decimated at the first Battle of the Somme on 1st July 1916. Plainly seen from the walk is the memorial cenotaph erected at the camp site.

Angram Cote Farm

O.S. MAPS :   Landranger Series (1 : 50 000) Sheet 99
(Northallerton and Ripon)
Pathfinder Series (1 : 25 000) Nº 630 (Sheet SE 17/18)
(Middleham and Jervaulx Abbey)

© Jack Keighley 1990

FREMINGTON EDGE & ARKLE BECK

7½ MILES

If you're looking for a walk with varied scenery then you won't find one to beat this, for the triangular route offers three totally contrasting sides. Lonely, heather-clad moors are crossed to Hurst, and the return by Arkle Beck is exquisitely sylvan. In between lies a scene of stark, utter desolation - a savagely mutilated landscape.

cairns on Fell End   *J Keighley*

45

PARKING In the centre of Reeth.
Map ref : 037 994

ROUTE DIRECTIONS ① ► Leave Reeth down the Richmond road. ② ► Immediately after crossing Reeth Bridge take a stile on the L and another just forward to the R. Cross the field ½ L to a gated stile at the wall corner, then follow the wall on the R. ③ ► Follow the tarmac lane for a few yards to a barn on the L, and here turn L into a rough lane. ④ ► Turn L up the next tarmac lane, which is now followed all the way to the top of Fremington Edge, although at White House the tarmac ends and the lane becomes a rough cart track. ⑤ ► Track forks. Keep R. ⑥ ► Beyond the gate a wide, stony track crosses the moor to Hurst. ⑦ ► At the hamlet turn L, and pass through two gates to a wide rough track rising through mining debris. Eventually this track curves through a line of grouse butts and becomes greener. As soon as a wall appears on the L, leave the track and cross heather to a gateway in an angle of the wall. ⑧ ► Go straight on towards more mining spoil, passing just to the L of it. 50 yds past a small cairn detour along a thin path to the cairns on Fell End. ⑨ ► Return to the original path and continue, aiming towards the prominent 'hush' across the valley ahead. On passing between two small ruins bear slightly L towards a hamlet across the valley. Look for a clear path coming down from the R and follow it as it heads back towards Fell End before turning very sharply R to descend to a gate and signpost. ⑩ ► Follow the wall on the R to descend to a farm lane by Strothwaite Hall. Turn L. ⑪ ► From a gate and BW sign cross two fields to reach Arkle Beck at a FB (don't cross it). ⑫ ► Leave the BW to follow a path by the beck (FP Reeth). Look out for waymarks (yellow blobs on tree trunks). ⑬ ► At a gap in a wall, two farms will be seen ahead. Make for the one on the R, going first to a wide gap stile in a wall corner. From the stile by the farm turn L (FP sign) and follow more waymarks, to rejoin the beck just beyond a ruined farm. ⑭ ► At a pair of gateposts forsake the main path for one alongside the beck. ⑮ ► At a crumbling wall the path

old chimney at Hurst

The setting of the tiny, isolated hamlet of Hurst is as bleak as anything in the Dales.

Lead was mined on these moors from Roman times to the turn of the present century. The chert quarries above White House produced a type of flint used in pottery making.

46

suddenly becomes a wide cart track climbing to the L. Leave it to go straight forward on a level grassy path. Soon a wire fence (which should have a stile but hasn't) bars the way. Climb alongside it for a few yards to an obvious crossing place, then descend, with care, to the path. ⑯ After passing along the lower edge of a belt of trees, take a stile on the L (easily missed) in a wall angle by a gate. Head straight across the field, but about ½ way across turn R to a stile marked with a white arrow. Continue parallel with the beck to join the outward route at point ②

derelict farm near Arkle Beck

The old market town of REETH is a good centre from which to explore both Swaledale and Arkengarthdale. A hundred years ago Reeth was an important lead-mining centre, with a much larger population than today. However, its shops and inns, grouped around the wide, sloping green, still retain an air of prosperity. At the lower end of the green a former Methodist schoolroom now houses the Swaledale Folk Museum, with a good range of exhibits illustrating the fascinating local history of the area. Reeth Bridge was built in 1773 by John Carr, the architect of Harewood House.

O.S. MAPS : Landranger Series (1:50 000) Sheets 98 (Wensleydale and Wharfedale) and 92 (Barnard Castle) Outdoor Leisure 30 (1:25 000) Yorkshire Dales (Northern and Central areas)

THE ASCENT OF WHERNSIDE
(FROM RIBBLEHEAD)

7½ MILES

This is the easiest and most interesting way up Yorkshire's highest mountain. The route follows Force Gill, with its delightful waterfalls, pools and cascades, to reach an extensive tarn (quite a rarity in the Dales). There follows a bracing walk, with magnificent views, along the mountain's eastern edge before descending to pleasing limestone scenery and gentle meadow paths.

Whernside from Batty Green

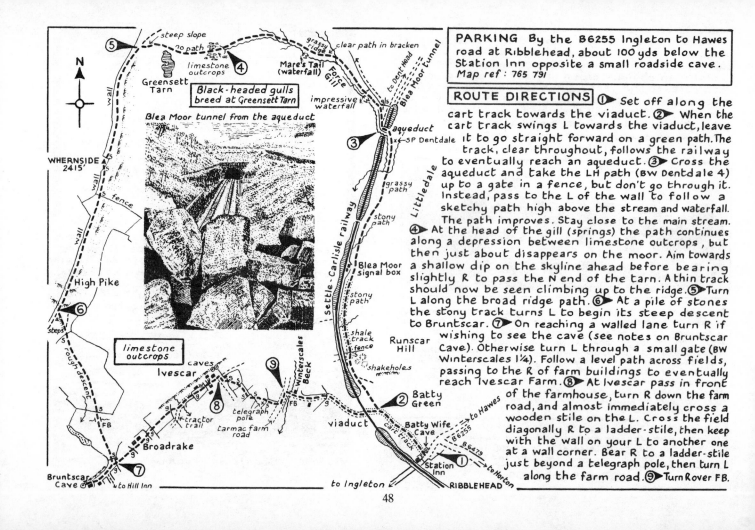

Map labels:

N

steep slope
no path
clear path in bracken

Greensett Tarn
limestone outcrops
⑤
④
Mare's Tail (waterfall)
Force Gill
grassy ridge
to Dent Head
Blea Moor tunnel

Black-headed gulls breed at Greensett Tarn

impressive waterfall

Blea Moor tunnel from the aqueduct

aqueduct
③
SP Dentdale

WHERNSIDE 2415'
wall
wall
fence

Littledale

grassy path
stony path

Settle–Carlisle railway

Blea Moor signal box

stony path

High Pike
⑥
steps

limestone outcrops

caves
Ivescar
⑧
③
⑨
Winterscales Beck
FB

Broadrake

Bruntscar Cave
⑦
to Hill Inn

shale track
fence
shakeholes

Runscar Hill

telegraph pole
tractor trail
tarmac farm road

FB

Batty Green
②

viaduct
Batty Wife Cave
cart track
Station Inn
①
B6255
B6479
to Hawes
to Horton

to Ingleton
RIBBLEHEAD

PARKING By the B6255 Ingleton to Hawes road at Ribblehead, about 100 yds below the Station Inn opposite a small roadside cave. Map ref: 765 791

ROUTE DIRECTIONS ① Set off along the cart track towards the viaduct. ② When the cart track swings L towards the viaduct, leave it to go straight forward on a green path. The track, clear throughout, follows the railway to eventually reach an aqueduct. ③ Cross the aqueduct and take the LH path (BW Dentdale 4) up to a gate in a fence, but don't go through it. Instead, pass to the L of the wall to follow a sketchy path high above the stream and waterfall. The path improves. Stay close to the main stream. ④ At the head of the gill (springs) the path continues along a depression between limestone outcrops, but then just about disappears on the moor. Aim towards a shallow dip on the skyline ahead before bearing slightly R to pass the N end of the tarn. A thin track should now be seen climbing up to the ridge. ⑤ Turn L along the broad ridge path. ⑥ At a pile of stones the stony track turns L to begin its steep descent to Bruntscar. ⑦ On reaching a walled lane turn R if wishing to see the cave (see notes on Bruntscar Cave). Otherwise turn L through a small gate (BW Winterscales 1¼). Follow a level path across fields, passing to the R of farm buildings to eventually reach Ivescar Farm. ⑧ At Ivescar pass in front of the farmhouse, turn R down the farm road, and almost immediately cross a wooden stile on the L. Cross the field diagonally R to a ladder-stile, then keep with the wall on your L to another one at a wall corner. Bear R to a ladder-stile just beyond a telegraph pole, then turn L along the farm road. ⑨ Turn Rover FB.

Although the highest of the famous 'Three Peaks', Whernside is the least shapely of the trio, from most directions appearing as a long, dull, whaleback sort of hump. The actual summit *summit* is none too exciting either, but the views across to Ingleborough and down Ribblesdale are quite superb. Railway freaks will enjoy the first two miles of the walk, and in the viaduct, aqueduct and tunnel will appreciate fine examples of Victorian engineering skill, enterprise and ingenuity. In mist a compass may be needed between points ④ and ⑤ on the walk.

BRUNTSCAR CAVE *is located in the scar immediately behind a house bearing the datestone '1689'. Access was formerly through a barn adjoining the house, but this is now in a dangerous state of collapse. The only approach is along the narrow gap between house and scar – a desperate scramble over rubble, slates and fallen masonry. Having survived this, the novice may confidently pass through the iron gate at the entrance and penetrate the cave for a considerable distance. Advice – carry* two *good torches.*

O.S. MAPS : Landranger Series (1 : 50 000) Sheet 98
(Wensleydale and Wharfedale)
Outdoor Leisure 2 (1 : 25 000) Yorkshire Dales
(Western area)

© Jack Keighley 1990

49

HARKERSIDE MOOR & APEDALE

8½ MILES

An invigorating walk on the windswept moors betwixt Wensleydale and Swaledale which will appeal to lovers of wild, lonely places. Although a height of just over 1800' is reached, at Apedale Head, much of the walking is level on excellent tracks and paths. There are magnificent views of Swaledale, and interesting remains of the mining activities of yesteryear.

shooting hut,
Browna Gill

J Keighley

49

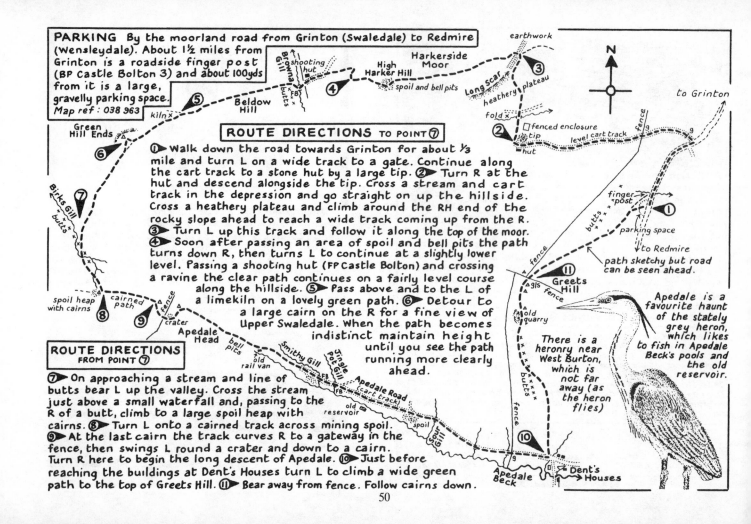

PARKING By the moorland road from Grinton (Swaledale) to Redmire (Wensleydale). About 1½ miles from Grinton is a roadside finger post (BP Castle Bolton 3) and about 100yds from it is a large, gravelly parking space. Map ref: 038 963

earthwork

Browna Gill · shooting hut · High Harker Hill · Harkerside Moor

Long Scar · heathery plateau · spoil and bell pits

fold

Beldow Hill · kiln

fenced enclosure · tip · level cart track · fence

hut

Green Hill Ends

to Grinton

N

finger post · butts · parking space · to Redmire

path sketchy but road can be seen ahead.

Birks Gill · butts

ROUTE DIRECTIONS TO POINT ⑦

① Walk down the road towards Grinton for about ⅓ mile and turn L on a wide track to a gate. Continue along the cart track to a stone hut by a large tip. ② Turn R at the hut and descend alongside the tip. Cross a stream and cart track in the depression and go straight on up the hillside. Cross a heathery plateau and climb around the RH end of the rocky slope ahead to reach a wide track coming up from the R. ③ Turn L up this track and follow it along the top of the moor. ④ Soon after passing an area of spoil and bell pits the path turns down R, then turns L to continue at a slightly lower level. Passing a shooting hut (FP Castle Bolton) and crossing a ravine the clear path continues on a fairly level course along the hillside. ⑤ Pass above and to the L of a limekiln on a lovely green path. ⑥ Detour to a large cairn on the R for a fine view of Upper Swaledale. When the path becomes indistinct maintain height until you see the path running more clearly ahead.

spoil heap with cairns · cairned path · fence · crater

Apedale Head · bell pits · old rail van · Smithy Gill · Jingle Pot Gill · FB · Apedale Road (cart track) · old reservoir · spoil · Sour Gill · Apedale Beck

Greets Hill · gls · fence · old quarry · butts · fence

There is a heronry near West Burton, which is not far away (as the heron flies)

Apedale is a favourite haunt of the stately grey heron, which likes to fish in Apedale Beck's pools and the old reservoir.

ROUTE DIRECTIONS FROM POINT ⑦

⑦ On approaching a stream and line of butts bear L up the valley. Cross the stream just above a small waterfall and, passing to the R of a butt, climb to a large spoil heap with cairns. ⑧ Turn L onto a cairned track across mining spoil. ⑨ At the last cairn the track curves R to a gateway in the fence, then swings L round a crater and down to a cairn. Turn R here to begin the long descent of Apedale. ⑩ Just before reaching the buildings at Dent's Houses turn L to climb a wide green path to the top of Greets Hill. ⑪ Bear away from fence. Follow cairns down.

Dent's Houses

LIMEKILNS

The kiln at Point ⑤

In the mid-18th century Dales farmers began to construct intake walls to enclose land on the edges of the moors. The new fields needed to be burned, drained and limed, and kilns were constructed to produce the huge amounts of lime required. The dry-stone masonry of the kiln had a funnel-shaped lining of brick or sandstone, and beneath the narrow neck at the bottom of this funnel was the grate for collecting lime and ash. A mixture of coal and limestone was fed into the top of the kiln and was fired by burning wood at the base. Once fired the kiln would usually be kept going for 2 or 3 days, by which time it would have produced some 30-40 tons of lime-enough to treat about 6-8 acres of land. Many farms had their own kilns, and some of the larger ones produced lime on a commercial basis. Limekilns had gone out of use by about 1860, but hundreds survive throughout the Dales. The large one seen on this walk is a very fine example.

The earthwork on Harkerside Moor is thought to date from the Iron Age (about 500 BC). Apedale's unusual name originates from a Norse name, Api — Api's dale.

The walk should be timed for late summer, when the heather is in bloom. More than most, the walk needs sunshine to highlight the colours. On a dull day it can look very dreary.

cairn on Green Hill Ends

O.S. MAPS : Landranger Series (1:50 000) Sheet 98
(Wensleydale and Wharfedale)
Outdoor Leisure 30 (1:25 000) Yorkshire Dales
(Northern and Central areas)

© Jack Keighley 1990

㊿

KETTLEWELL & STARBOTTON

5 MILES

A fairly gentle stroll in a lovely and popular stretch of Wharfedale. The walk to Starbotton makes use of a level limestone terrace only slightly elevated from the valley floor. The return route along the steeper and craggier western side of the dale provides fine views as it climbs to a height of almost 1250 feet.

Fox and Hounds Starbotton

J. Keighley

①► From the car park go over the bridge *into* the village and take the lane immediately to the L of the Bluebell Hotel. When this lane turns R go straight on up a path between walls. ②► At the top of the walled section turn L at the wall corner. The path now runs clear and practically level all the way to Starbotton, with a wall close by on the L almost throughout. ③► To descend to Starbotton turn L through a metal gate into a field with a barn and bear R down through a gateway to reach a gate leading out onto a lane. ④► Turn L down to the main road, and cross it to a walled path (BW Arncliffe 2¼ FP Kettlewell 2 FP Buckden 2¼). ⑤► When the path forks keep L (straight on) down to the river bridge. ⑥► Across the bridge go straight forward (SP Arncliffe) along a path between remains of old walls. Turn L round behind an old barn where the path begins its long steady climb up the fellside. After passing through a wood the clear, stony track continues to rise until it reaches a gate and stile in a crosswall. ⑦► Cross the stile and turn L (SP Kettlewell) alongside the wall to another stile. Stay on a level course across two more fields, heading towards the buildings of Moor End. ⑧► About 100yds from the end of the second field turn R up to a stile in the wall, which carries a notice (Trial Diversion). Through this stile turn L and follow the wall to a metal gate leading into the field at Moor End. Pass in front of the house and turn R to a gate by an outbuilding. (Note: Beware of the barbed wire wound around the top of this and subsequent gates. The author once ripped his hand open here). ⑨► Go forward along a grass path with a wall on the L. On passing through a gate the path develops into a rough cart-track, crossing a small ravine before steeply zig-zagging down to the L to come alongside a wall which is followed via three gates to the main road. Turn L over the bridge to the car park.

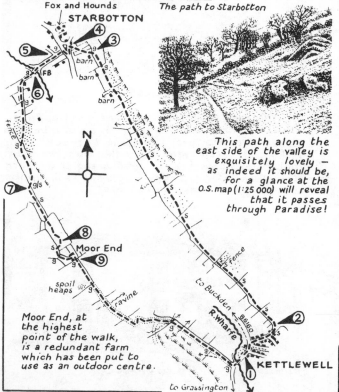

The path to Starbotton

This path along the east side of the valley is exquisitely lovely — as indeed it should be, for a glance at the O.S. map (1:25 000) will reveal that it passes through Paradise!

Moor End, at the highest point of the walk, is a redundant farm which has been put to use as an outdoor centre.

The steep sides and very gently-curved floor of the dale are typical features of a glaciated valley, seen to good effect in the view from point ⑦. The riverside fields hereabouts are liable to widespread flooding.

The little grey village of KETTLEWELL, with its splendid old houses clustered around the beck, was a thriving market town as long ago as the 13th. century. During the 18th. and 19th. centuries Kettlewell took over a new role as a lead-mining village, and its three old inns indicate that it was also a recognised stopping place for stagecoaches in those days. Now Kettlewell is a magnet for tourists in general and walkers in particular; it is an ideal base for a holiday in the Dales.

Kettlewell

STARBOTTON, nearly three miles up the valley from Kettlewell, is a charming little village. Many of its old cottages have been attractively and tastefully restored and modernised. The focal point of the village is the Fox and Hounds Inn, a welcoming and convivial little pub which dispenses a good pint. Starbotton was almost completely destroyed in 1686, for in that fateful year a terrible thunderstorm brought raging flood waters down Cam Gill, causing utter devastation. Prior to this the village had some importance as a crossroads of packhorse routes, and it was here that travellers from Ribblesdale and Littondale crossed the Wharfe on their way via the Walden Road to Wensleydale.

O.S. MAPS :   Landranger Series (1 : 50 000) Sheet 98
                        (Wensleydale and Wharfedale)
                Outdoor Leisure 30 (1 : 25 000) Yorkshire Dales
                        (Northern and Central areas)
                © Jack Keighley 1990

WALKS IN THE YORKSHIRE DALES

(51)

ILKLEY MOOR

(HEADGEAR OPTIONAL)

6½ MILES

A bracing walk on ancient trackways along the edge of what is perhaps the most famous piece of moorland in Britain. The route, besides offering panoramic views of Lower Wharfedale, visits a whole succession of places and objects of interest. The rugged gritstone scenery in the vicinity of Ilkley Crags is quite magnificent.

Cow and Calf Rocks

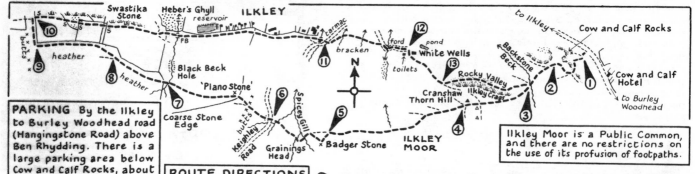

Ilkley Moor is a Public Common, and there are no restrictions on the use of its profusion of footpaths.

ROUTE DIRECTIONS

① From the car park walk up the stepped path towards the big square opening in the crags, but before reaching it turn L up another stepped path. At the top of the climb turn R to follow a broad path along the top of the crags. **②** On coming to a large quarry with fir trees, bear L onto a wide path heading across the depression towards the high skyline. **③** Cross a rocky stream and take the L of two paths climbing the moor. (The RH path, which leads to Rocky Valley, will be our return route). Cross a cairned track and continue up to the big heap of stones atop Cranshaw Thorn Hill. **④** Choose the middle of three paths to continue straight ahead on a fairly level course. Ignore any tracks going off to the R, and when the path forks bear L, climbing slightly towards two masts on the skyline before the clear path gradually veers R. **⑤** Detour to visit the Badger Stone (with a seat by it) on the L, then return to the main path to cross the head of a gill and reach a rough-metalled road. **⑥** Across the road two wooden stumps indicate the start of a path up the moor. On reaching grouse butts bear slightly R to a boulder shaped like an open grand piano. Continue forward on a level path, then descend slightly to cross a stream. **⑦** Go through a gap in the wall and follow a path running parallel with the wall on the R. **⑧** As the wall disappears from view the path forks. Keep R to rejoin the wall **⑨** Turn R at the wall corner and follow the wall down. **⑩** Turn R through a stile in the wall onto a clear path along the edge of the moor. After passing the Swastika Stone keep immediately to the R of a wood and a reservoir. **⑪** Cross the tarmac road and turn L down a path in the bracken running parallel with the road. The path eventually swings R and a prominent white building (White Wells) comes into view ahead. **⑫** Turn R up the path immediately to the R of White Wells, and climb fairly steeply up the moor. **⑬** About 50 yds before reaching a stepped section of the path turn L onto a narrower path, which soon widens as it enters Rocky Valley. Keep on it to join the outward route at point ③.

The 'Piano Stone' above the Keighley Road

WHITE WELLS was built by Squire Middleton in the eighteenth century as a bath-house for the people of Ilkley, who could there enjoy a dip in the cold but pure and supposedly curative waters of the moorland spring. The house was restored during the 1970s, and is open to the public as a museum and visitor centre.

Many of the rocks and boulders on these moors bear strange carvings which date back to the Bronze Age. Most common are the 'cup and ring' markings — small hollows within a circle or concentric circles. The BADGER STONE has an elaborate design carved on its south face, although it is badly eroded and was damaged by battle practice during the Second World War. The famous SWASTIKA STONE, protected from vandalism by iron railings, displays a rounded version of the ancient good luck symbol, which is also incorporated in the design on the Badger Stone. The moor edge track is thought to have been part of an important Bronze Age trade route. COW AND CALF ROCKS, a famous and popular attraction much-frequented by rock-climbers, bear no resemblance whatsoever to the animals whose names they carry. HEBERS GHYLL is a wooded ravine delightfully laid out with paths, steps and little footbridges.

carving on the Swastika Stone

O.S. MAPS : Landranger Series (1 : 50 000) Sheet 104
(Leeds, Bradford and Harrogate)
Pathfinder Series (1 : 25 000) Nº 671 Sheet SE 04/14
(Keighley and Ilkley)

© Jack Keighley 1990

52

FORELANDS RIGG

5¾ MILES

Forelands Rigg is the north-eastern extremity of Wasset Fell, which divides the lower reaches of Walden and Bishopdale. Starting from West Burton's beautiful waterfall, this unusual walk visits each of these lovely side-valleys of Wensleydale, and in doing so takes us through the silent forest which drapes the intervening ridge.

Burton Force

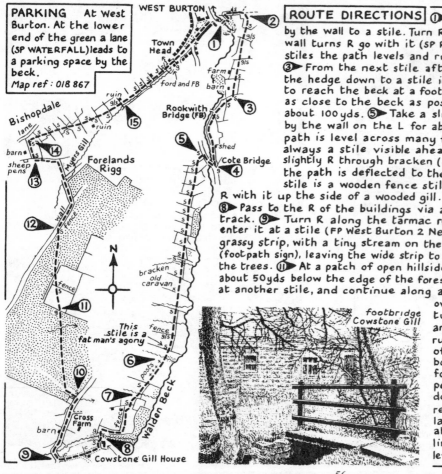

PARKING At West Burton. At the lower end of the green a lane (SP WATERFALL) leads to a parking space by the beck.
Map ref: 018 867

WEST BURTON

Town Head

farm

ford and FB

ruin

Bishopdale lane

ruin

Myers Gill

Forelands Rigg

barn

sheep pens

wall fence

This stile is a fat man's agony

fence

bracken old caravan

Rookwith Bridge (FB)

shed

Cote Bridge

posts

Walden Beck

fence

Cross Farm

barn

Cowstone Gill House

N

footbridge Cowstone Gill

ROUTE DIRECTIONS ① Cross the footbridge and turn sharp L up by the wall to a stile. Turn R and climb alongside the wall. ② When the wall turns R go with it (SP Rookwith Bridge, Cote Bridge). After two more stiles the path levels and runs parallel with the wooded gill on the R. ③ From the next stile after passing a barn on the R turn R to follow the hedge down to a stile in the corner, then cross the field diagonally to reach the beck at a footbridge. Don't cross it. Walk upstream keeping as close to the beck as possible. ④ Turn R along the tarmac road for about 100 yds. ⑤ Take a slit stile on the L (FP Cowstone Gill 1½). Go up by the wall on the L for about 80 yds to a stile in it. From here the path is level across many fields. It is not always clear, but there is always a stile visible ahead. ⑥ After a very narrow stile the path bears slightly R through bracken (marker posts). ⑦ On crossing a small stream the path is deflected to the R by a wall corner. Just beyond the next stile is a wooden fence stile. Don't cross this. Follow the fence, turning R with it up the side of a wooded gill. At the crosswall turn L down to a footbridge. ⑧ Pass to the R of the buildings via a stile in the wall, then turn R up the farm track. ⑨ Turn R along the tarmac road. ⑩ When the roadside forest is reached enter it at a stile (FP West Burton 2 Newbiggin 1). Go straight up a wide, unplanted, grassy strip, with a tiny stream on the L. After about 150 yds the path turns ½ R, (footpath sign), leaving the wide strip to run along a much narrower defile through the trees. ⑪ At a patch of open hillside bear slightly L to find a stile in the fence about 50 yds below the edge of the forest. Maintain direction to enter the forest at another stile, and continue along another narrow defile (initially somewhat overgrown). ⑫ At the edge of the forest turn R along the grassy strip between wall and fence, and stay with it as it turns L to run down by the trees. At the bottom corner of the forest keep straight on down to the bottom of the next field, and here turn L to follow the wall. ⑬ Just before some sheep pens, turn R through a stile and go straight down the field alongside a wall. ⑭ When you reach an isolated stile (just before a walled lane) turn R and make for a stile in the wall ahead. From here the path runs through a line of slit stiles (just for a change), and is level or slightly uphill. ⑮ At a ruined barn the path comes alongside a stream on the R. Follow it to a footbridge and go straight on through the farmyard into West Burton.

STILES

If you like stiles (which the author does, finding them reassuring) and you have a sylph-like figure (which the author does not) you will enjoy this walk. There are nearly fifty stiles *en route* (although some need not be used as they stand alongside open gates or gaps in broken walls), and the vast majority are of the narrow slit variety.

Stile near Town Head

The dale running south from West Burton is properly called WALDEN, although it is often referred to as Waldendale or The Walden Valley. It is a quiet and beautiful valley with no through motor route. Two narrow lanes penetrate the dale on opposite sides of the beck but do not connect. The name 'Walden' derives from 'weala'(a Welshman or foreigner) and 'denu'(a valley). In the Middle Ages the terms 'Welshman' and 'foreigner' were synonymous. Walden Beck rises on Buckden Pike and flows for a good seven miles to reach West Burton.

BISHOPDALE is the largest of Wensleydale's many tributary valleys, and is about a mile wide at its foot, where the villages of Thoralby and Newbiggin face each other across the dale. Many thousands of years ago Bishopdale contained a large glacial lake, and the deposited silt has given the valley a fertile soil.

The attractive village of West Burton is fortunate in lying just off the main motor roads.

houses at West Burton

O.S. MAPS : Landranger Series (1 : 50 000) Sheet 98
(Wensleydale and Wharfedale)
Outdoor Leisure 30 (1 : 25 000) Yorkshire Dales
(Northern and Central areas)

© Jack Keighley 1990

53

THE ASCENT OF BUCKDEN PIKE
(FROM BUCKDEN)

7½ MILES

A very popular walk offering a wide variety of terrain and scenery. After visiting the top of Yorkshire's sixth highest fell, there are superb views of Upper Wharfedale as a splendid descent is made, down an ancient drovers' track, to the little village of Starbotton. The easy riverside return follows an attractive section of the much-trodden Dales Way.

Buckden — J Keighley

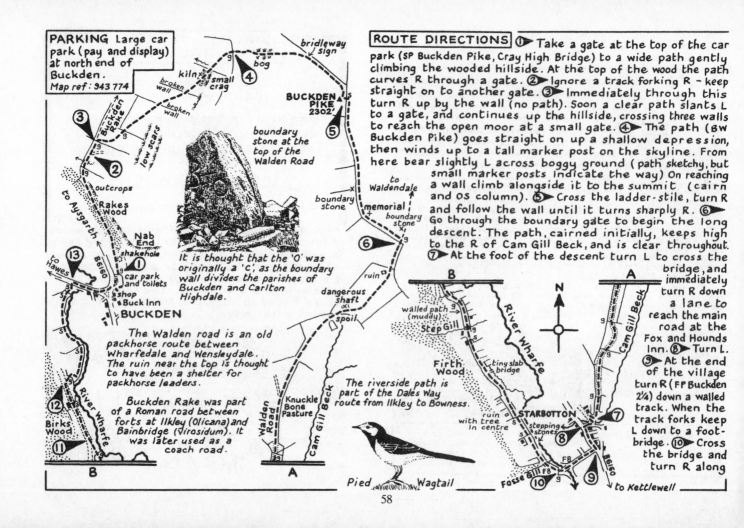

bridleway sign

bog

kiln small crag

3

Buckden Rake

BUCKDEN PIKE 2302'

boundary stone at the top of the Walden Road

2

low scars

to Aysgarth

outcrops

Rakes Wood

Nab End shakehole

13

B6160

to Hawes

car park and toilets

shop
Buck Inn

BUCKDEN

boundary stone

to Waldendale

memorial

boundary stone

5

6

ruin

dangerous shaft

spoil

It is thought that the 'O' was originally a 'C', as the boundary wall divides the parishes of Buckden and Carlton Highdale.

The Walden road is an old packhorse route between Wharfedale and Wensleydale. The ruin near the top is thought to have been a shelter for packhorse leaders.

Buckden Rake was part of a Roman road between forts at Ilkley (Olicana) and Bainbridge (Virosidum). It was later used as a coach road.

12

Birks Wood

11

River Wharfe

B

Walden Road

Knuckle Bone Pasture

Cam Gill Beck

The riverside path is part of the Dales Way route from Ilkley to Bowness.

Pied Wagtail

A

walled path (muddy)

Step Gill

Firth Wood

tiny slab bridge

ruin with tree in centre

STARBOTTON

stepping stones

8

Fosse Gill

10

FB

FB

9

B6160

B

River Wharfe

N

A

Cam Gill Beck

7

to Kettlewell

ROUTE DIRECTIONS ① Take a gate at the top of the car park (SP Buckden Pike, Cray High Bridge) to a wide path gently climbing the wooded hillside. At the top of the wood the path curves R through a gate. ② Ignore a track forking R – keep straight on to another gate. ③ Immediately through this turn R up by the wall (no path). Soon a clear path slants L to a gate, and continues up the hillside, crossing three walls to reach the open moor at a small gate. ④ The path (BW Buckden Pike) goes straight on up a shallow depression, then winds up to a tall marker post on the skyline. From here bear slightly L across boggy ground (path sketchy, but small marker posts indicate the way) On reaching a wall climb alongside it to the summit (cairn and OS column). ⑤ Cross the ladder-stile, turn R and follow the wall until it turns sharply R. ⑥ Go through the boundary gate to begin the long descent. The path, cairned initially, keeps high to the R of Cam Gill Beck, and is clear throughout. ⑦ At the foot of the descent turn L to cross the bridge, and immediately turn R down a lane to reach the main road at the Fox and Hounds Inn. ⑧ Turn L. ⑨ At the end of the village turn R (FP Buckden 2¼) down a walled track. When the track forks keep L down to a foot-bridge. ⑩ Cross the bridge and turn R along the riverside path. When the river bends away to the R the clear, waymarked path continues straight ahead, with a wall on the L. ⑪ With the river now close again, the path joins a wide track. ⑫ About 150 yds past a large barn turn R (footpath sign) down a narrow path to a gate. Descend to the riverside path and follow it upstream to Buckden Bridge. ⑬ Turn R along the road.

LONE SURVIVOR....

On the 31st January 1942 an R.A.F. plane, crewed by six Polish airmen, crashed on Buckden Pike in a blizzard. One man, badly injured but the sole survivor, crawled from the wreckage to find, nearby, the prints of a fox in the snow.

He followed the tracks downhill, and eventually they led him to a farm and safety.

He later erected this cross at the scene of the crash, in thanksgiving for his escape and in memory of the five men who died.

Below the inscription he placed a bronze fox's head, and fragments of the wreckage are set into the concrete base.

BUCKDEN was, in medieval times, the headquarters of the foresters of Langstrothdale Chase, and takes its name from the deer which roamed the countryside in those days.

BUCKDEN PIKE is not really a pike at all, having a flat and extensive (and wet!) summit plateau. It is, however, an excellent viewpoint, and the walk should be reserved for a clear day

O.S. MAPS : Landranger Series (1:50 000) Sheet 98
(Wensleydale and Wharfedale)
Outdoor Leisure 30 (1:25 000) Yorkshire Dales
(Northern and Central areas)

© Jack Keighley 1990

KELD WATERFALLS & WHITSUNDALE

7¼ MILES

Upper Swaledale is grand walking country, and its wild beauty will be appreciated to the full on this varied and richly satisfying ramble. The crossing of the lonely foothills of Great Shunner Fell provides a marked contrast to the dramatic river scenery encountered at the start and finish of the walk. Magnificent views.

Kisdon Force   J Keighley

Stile and barn   Whitsundale

PARKING Can be a problem, especially at weekends and Bank Holidays. If possible, park in the square at the bottom of Keld village, just off the B6270 Muker to Kirkby Stephen road.

Map ref: 893 012
Failing this, you may find an odd space alongside the B6270.

ROUTE DIRECTIONS

① Leave Keld by the walled track (Public Footpath to Muker). ② When the track forks (both branches signposted 'Pennine Way') turn L down to the river. Cross the bridge and go up the path to the L of the falls to a cart track. Go L along it up to the farm. ③ Bear L through the farmyard and leave along the farm road. ④ Turn L down the motor road. ⑤ At the sharp L bend go up to a stile in a fence (Raven Seat 2). Climb the clear path up to a wall and turn L alongside it. The path now runs along the top of the scar, with a fence on the L. ⑥ Go L through a gap in the wall and turn R up the cart track. ⑦ When the cart track ends at a barn continue forward on a green path, aiming towards a distant post. The path fades, but on passing to the L of a large fold becomes clear again, and remains clear all the way up the valley to the farm at Ravenseat. ⑧ Turn L down to the hump bridge and head back down the valley on the tarmac farm road. ⑨ Just past Black Howe, where the road becomes unenclosed, turn L down by the wall to a ladder-stile. Keep on down past a barn to a stile just to the R of another barn. ⑩ Make for the RH barn of two seen ahead, using a stile to pass to the R of it. Keep straight on downhill to reach the main road. ⑪ Turn L, and immediately you have crossed the bridge take a gate on the R (footpath sign), and climb the steep slope to a ladder-stile in the wall on the L. A thin track now continues, rising gently and crossing two ladder-stiles before descending to a stream. ⑫ Cross the stream and maintain direction, climbing to locate a stile in the wall ahead, from which a clear path continues to another stile. ⑬ Follow a track by a wall at the foot of a heather slope. After about 200 yards turn R through a slit stile and continue forward, bearing slightly away from the wall and climbing gently to reach a broad green path. Bear L to locate a stile in a crosswall, then continue forward

Map labels

B   A   ⑦
barn   farm   ⑥
barn   Cotterby Scar
motor road to Tan Hill
Currack Force
R. Swale   ⑪   Low Bridge   Wain Wath Force
⑤ Park Bridge   ④ Rainby Force
farm road   PW   East Stonesdale
Ravenseat   High Bridge
F.B. and ford   ⑧   heather
fold   track   Blackburn Beck
butts   ⑫
barns   heather slope   ⑬
Whitsundale   tarmac farm road
Black Howe   Howgate Scars
⑨   barn   ⑨   Oven Mouth   Ay Gill   ⑲
⑩   barn   barn   large fold   ⑱   gorse   ⑰
signpost   N   ⑭   kiln   ⑯
B   A   Angram   ⑮
Catrake Force
KELD   ③
Y.H.A.   B6270   East Gill Force
①   Kisdon Force
②

Before crossing the stile at point ⑤, detour down to the bridge for a view upstream of Wain Wath Force.

through another stile and down by a wall to a gate. ⑭
From the gate bear slightly L, and when Angram appears
go down to it on a path between walls. ⑮ Turn L along
the road, and in 100 yards turn R through a gate (FP Keld).
Go down by the wall on the R and near the bottom of the
slope bear L to a gate. ⑯ Bear L again to a stile by a tall
tree, then climb steeply up the next field to a stile in
its far corner, from there turning R up to a small gate.
⑰ Turn L and follow the wall. Continue along a walled
path. ⑱ Cross a wide stony track to a gate up on the R,
then follow a clear path, passing to the R of a barn. ⑲
On passing through a gap at a wall corner, keep to the LH
edge of the next field, and at the bottom of it cross a
stile on the L. Follow the field boundary on the R. Turn R
through a gate and L(✱) through another on the main path
back to Keld. ✱ For a short detour to see Kisdon Force, turn R
here, and in a few yards you will come to a signposted path. But
take care – the path is narrow and slippery above a precipitous
slope. Definitely not a place for larking about.

The walk up Whitsundale to Ravenseat (a
remote cluster of farm buildings) takes us
high above a spectacular gorge and past
some sparkling waterfalls
and cascades. Beyond
Ravenseat, however, the
scenery is very bleak.

The return route to Keld
from High Bridge onward
has many ups and downs
and is quite strenuous.
If running short of time
or energy, or if the weather
turns nasty, you could go
back by the main road – 1½
miles to Keld.

Ravenseat

O.S. MAPS : Landranger Series (1 : 50 000) Either Sheet 91 (Appleby-in
-Westmorland) or Sheet 92 (Barnard Castle) contain all
but a very tiny section at Angram (Sheet 98)
Outdoor Leisure 30 (1 : 25 000) Yorkshire Dales (Northern and Central)

© Jack Keighley 1990

61

BORDLEY TOWN

7½ MILES

Set in the peaceful, rolling hills between
Grassington and Malham, this typical Dales
walk is one of marked contrasts. The southern
section is exquisitely beautiful, whilst to the
north the route traverses bare and windswept
uplands. Caves and potholes, a 'forgotten' village
and a classic drovers' road are just some of the
many highlights met along the way.

Mastiles Lane

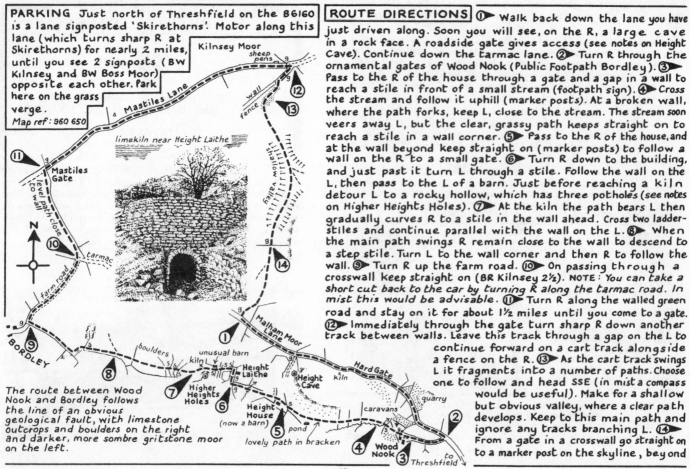

PARKING Just north of Threshfield on the B6160 is a lane signposted 'Skirethorns'. Motor along this lane (which turns sharp R at Skirethorns) for nearly 2 miles, until you see 2 signposts (BW Kilnsey and BW Boss Moor) opposite each other. Park here on the grass verge.

Map ref: 960 650

Kilnsey Moor

sheep pens

Mastiles Lane

wall fence

limekiln near Height Laithe

Mastiles Gate

level path close to wall

N

tarmac

farm road

shallow valley

Malham Moor Lane

BORDLEY

boulders

unusual barn

kiln

Height Laithe

Hard Gate

kiln

Height Cave

quarry

Higher Heights Holes

Height House (now a barn)

pond

caravans

lovely path in bracken

Wood Nook

to Threshfield

The route between Wood Nook and Bordley follows the line of an obvious geological fault, with limestone outcrops and boulders on the right and darker, more sombre gritstone moor on the left.

ROUTE DIRECTIONS ① Walk back down the lane you have just driven along. Soon you will see, on the R, a large cave in a rock face. A roadside gate gives access (see notes on Height Cave). Continue down the tarmac lane. ② Turn R through the ornamental gates of Wood Nook (Public Footpath Bordley). ③ Pass to the R of the house through a gate and a gap in a wall to reach a stile in front of a small stream (footpath sign). ④ Cross the stream and follow it uphill (marker posts). At a broken wall, where the path forks, keep L, close to the stream. The stream soon veers away L, but the clear, grassy path keeps straight on to reach a stile in a wall corner. ⑤ Pass to the R of the house, and at the wall beyond keep straight on (marker posts) to follow a wall on the R to a small gate. ⑥ Turn R down to the building, and just past it turn L through a stile. Follow the wall on the L, then pass to the L of a barn. Just before reaching a kiln detour L to a rocky hollow, which has three potholes (see notes on Higher Heights Holes). ⑦ At the kiln the path bears L then gradually curves R to a stile in the wall ahead. Cross two ladder-stiles and continue parallel with the wall on the L. ⑧ When the main path swings R remain close to the wall to descend to a step stile. Turn L to the wall corner and then R to follow the wall. ⑨ Turn R up the farm road. ⑩ On passing through a crosswall keep straight on (BR Kilnsey 2½). NOTE: You can take a short cut back to the car by turning R along the tarmac road. In mist this would be advisable. ⑪ Turn R along the walled green road and stay on it for about 1½ miles until you come to a gate. ⑫ Immediately through the gate turn sharp R down another track between walls. Leave this track through a gap on the L to continue forward on a cart track alongside a fence on the R. ⑬ As the cart track swings L it fragments into a number of paths. Choose one to follow and head SSE (in mist a compass would be useful). Make for a shallow but obvious valley, where a clear path develops. Keep to this main path and ignore any tracks branching L. ⑭ From a gate in a crosswall go straight on to a marker post on the skyline, beyond which a clear path descends to our starting point.

BORDLEY is as small as a hamlet could possibly be — just two farms - but in the middle ages it was large enough to have the status of a 'township', and is still sometimes referred to as 'Bordley Town' by local people. It was a grange of Fountains Abbey, and stood at an important 'route crossroads' in medieval times. MASTILES LANE is a classic 'green road' — the most famous of all the many old drovers' roads in the Dales. It was part of a busy medieval highway between Fountains Abbey and the Lake District.

two views of the 'unusual barn'

The cave shown as HEIGHT CAVE on the O.S. map has several alternative names (Heights Cave, Skythorns Cave, Calf Hole, Elland Cave). There is no right-of-way to it, but it's only about 150 yards from the road, and as long as you close the gate and leave no litter there should be no problem. It is an impressive place - a large chamber with twin entrances split by a rock pillar. Various Iron- and Bronze-age tools and weapons have been found here, some of which can be seen at the Craven Museum in Skipton.

O.S. MAPS :   Landranger Series (1:50 000) Sheet 98
(Wensleydale and Wharfedale)
Outdoor Leisure 10 (1:25 000) Yorkshire Dales
(Southern area)

PIKE HILL & HARDRAW FORCE

7¼ MILES

An Upper Wensleydale walk of great variety and charm, with sweeping views of the dale from the fine high-level traverse above Sedbusk. The ideal time to do the walk is late spring, when the woods at Hardraw are at their loveliest, and preferably after a spell of wet weather has enhanced the display of England's highest waterfall.

Haylands Bridge   JKeighley

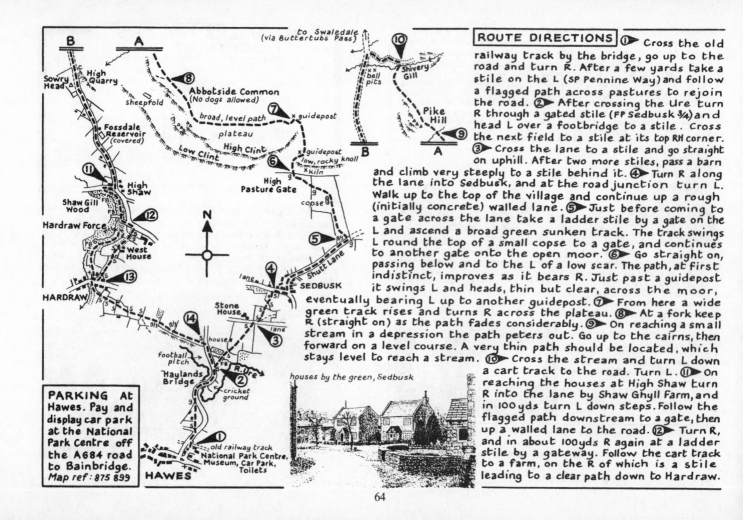

B | **A**

High Quarry

Sowry Head

sheepfold

⑧ Abbotside Common
(No dogs allowed)

⑩ Shivery Gill

Pike Hill

bell pits

broad, level path ⑦ × guidepost

plateau

Fossdale Reservoir (covered)

High Clint

Low Clint

⑪

⑥ × guidepost
low, rocky knoll
× Kiln

B

⑨ **A**

High Shaw

Shaw Gill Wood

High Pasture Gate

copse

⑫

Hardraw Force

West House

⑤ g/s

Shutt Lane

⑬

lane ④

SEDBUSK

HARDRAW

lane

Stone House

⑭

house

③

football pitch

R. Ure

Haylands Bridge

②

cricket ground

N

① old railway track
National Park Centre, Museum, Car Park, Toilets

HAWES

ROUTE DIRECTIONS

⓪ Cross the old railway track by the bridge, go up to the road and turn R. After a few yards take a stile on the L (SP Pennine Way) and follow a flagged path across pastures to rejoin the road. ② After crossing the Ure turn R through a gated stile (FP Sedbusk ¾) and head L over a footbridge to a stile. Cross the next field to a stile at its top RH corner. ③ Cross the lane to a stile and go straight on uphill. After two more stiles, pass a barn and climb very steeply to a stile behind it. ④ Turn R along the lane into Sedbusk, and at the road junction turn L. Walk up to the top of the village and continue up a rough (initially concrete) walled lane. ⑤ Just before coming to a gate across the lane take a ladder stile by a gate on the L and ascend a broad green sunken track. The track swings L round the top of a small copse to a gate, and continues to another gate onto the open moor. ⑥ Go straight on, passing below and to the L of a low scar. The path, at first indistinct, improves as it bears R. Just past a guidepost it swings L and heads, thin but clear, across the moor, eventually bearing L up to another guidepost. ⑦ From here a wide green track rises and turns R across the plateau. ⑧ At a fork keep R (straight on) as the path fades considerably. ⑨ On reaching a small stream in a depression the path peters out. Go up to the cairns, then forward on a level course. A very thin path should be located, which stays level to reach a stream. ⑩ Cross the stream and turn L down a cart track to the road. Turn L. ⑪ On reaching the houses at High Shaw turn R into the lane by Shaw Ghyll Farm, and in 100yds turn L down steps. Follow the flagged path downstream to a gate, then up a walled lane to the road. ⑫ Turn R, and in about 100yds R again at a ladder stile by a gateway. Follow the cart track to a farm, on the R of which is a stile leading to a clear path down to Hardraw.

houses by the green, Sedbusk

⑬► After visiting the waterfall (see notes) take the Pennine Way path immediately to the R of the shop opposite the Green Dragon. Behind the buildings bear L onto a flagged path. ⑭► At the road turn R to rejoin the outward route at point ②.

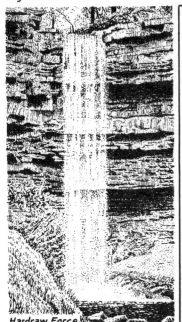
Hardraw Force

HARDRAW FORCE falls in a single leap of 96 feet at the head of a wooded limestone gorge. The land is privately owned, and the only access is through the Green Dragon Inn, where a charge is made. The gorge has remarkable acoustics, and a bandstand at its entrance dates from Victorian times, when annual brass band contests were held here. The event has recently been revived. The rock wall behind the waterfall reveals strata of the 'Yoredale cycle.' At the top is hard black limestone, forming a considerable over-hang. At the foot are beds of shale, and the middle section consists of layers of sandstone. Because of the overhang one can walk behind the fall and return down the R bank of the stream to a foot-bridge. The French stuntman Charles Blondin once walked over the waterfall on a tightrope, pausing midway to cook an omelette.

O.S. MAPS :   Landranger Series (1 : 50 000) Sheet 98
(Wensleydale and Wharfedale)
Outdoor Leisure 30 (1 : 25 000) Yorkshire Dales
(Northern and Central areas)

57

A CANALSIDE WALK FROM GARGRAVE

7 MILES

And now for something completely different .... a stroll along the towpath of the Leeds - Liverpool Canal, with a return to Gargrave through the lush green pastures of one of the most rural sections of the Pennine Way. Be sure to do the walk in high summer, when the canal is busy with colourful holiday craft.

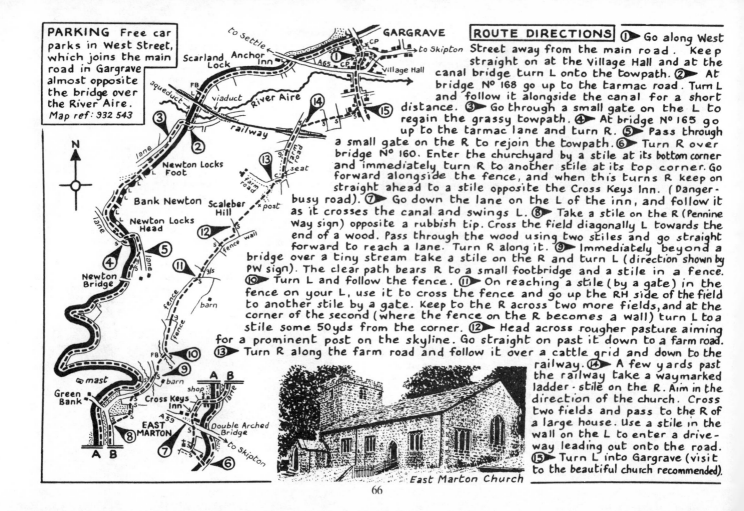

N

to Settle

Scarland Lock

Anchor Inn

GARGRAVE

CP

to Skipton

Village Hall

aqueduct

FB

viaduct

River Aire

lane

railway

③

②

Newton Locks Foot

Bank Newton

Scaleber Hill

Newton Locks Head

⑬

farm road

post

seat

lane

lane

⑫

fence wall

⑤

④

Newton Bridge

⑪

fence

fence

barn

FB

⑩

⑨

barn

mast

Green Bank

shop

Cross Keys Inn

EAST MARTON

⑧

⑦

A B

A B

Double Arched Bridge

to Skipton

⑥

⑭

⑮

A65

A59

ROUTE DIRECTIONS

① Go along West Street away from the main road. Keep straight on at the Village Hall and at the canal bridge turn L onto the towpath. ② At bridge Nº 168 go up to the tarmac road. Turn L and follow it alongside the canal for a short distance. ③ Go through a small gate on the L to regain the grassy towpath. ④ At bridge Nº 165 go up to the tarmac lane and turn R. ⑤ Pass through a small gate on the R to rejoin the towpath. ⑥ Turn R over bridge Nº 160. Enter the churchyard by a stile at its bottom corner and immediately turn R to another stile at its top corner. Go forward alongside the fence, and when this turns R keep on straight ahead to a stile opposite the Cross Keys Inn. (Danger - busy road). ⑦ Go down the lane on the L of the inn, and follow it as it crosses the canal and swings L. ⑧ Take a stile on the R (Pennine Way sign) opposite a rubbish tip. Cross the field diagonally L towards the end of a wood. Pass through the wood using two stiles and go straight forward to reach a lane. Turn R along it. ⑨ Immediately beyond a bridge over a tiny stream take a stile on the R and turn L (direction shown by PW sign). The clear path bears R to a small footbridge and a stile in a fence. ⑩ Turn L and follow the fence. ⑪ On reaching a stile (by a gate) in the fence on your L, use it to cross the fence and go up the RH side of the field to another stile by a gate. Keep to the R across two more fields, and at the corner of the second (where the fence on the R becomes a wall) turn L to a stile some 50yds from the corner. ⑫ Head across rougher pasture aiming for a prominent post on the skyline. Go straight on past it down to a farm road. ⑬ Turn R along the farm road and follow it over a cattle grid and down to the railway. ⑭ A few yards past the railway take a waymarked ladder-stile on the R. Aim in the direction of the church. Cross two fields and pass to the R of a large house. Use a stile in the wall on the L to enter a drive-way leading out onto the road. ⑮ Turn L into Gargrave (visit to the beautiful church recommended).

East Marton Church

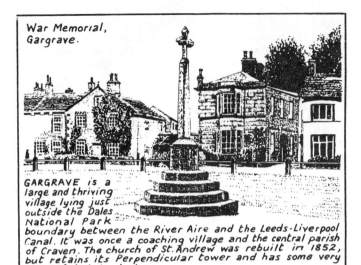

War Memorial, Gargrave.

GARGRAVE is a large and thriving village lying just outside the Dales National Park boundary between the River Aire and the Leeds-Liverpool Canal. It was once a coaching village and the central parish of Craven. The church of St. Andrew was rebuilt in 1852, but retains its Perpendicular tower and has some very beautiful stained glass.

The construction of the LEEDS – LIVERPOOL CANAL, authorised by Act of Parliament in 1770, took more than 20 years. Notice how, between Newton Bridge and East Marton, the canal makes big sweeping bends in order to contour the land and thus avoid the use of locks. Even so there are over 90 locks along the full course of the canal. The waterway reaches its most northerly point at Gargrave, and its highest point (nearly 500′) a few miles beyond East Marton.

O.S. MAPS :   Landranger Series (1 : 50 000) Sheet 103
                                    (Blackburn and Burnley)
              Pathfinder Series (1 : 25 000) Sheet SD 85/95
                                    (Skipton and Hellifield)
✴ Note : All the route except for a small section at the southern
tip is shown on Outdoor Leisure 10 (1 : 25 000) Y. Dales (Southern area)

© Jack Keighley 1990

58

AROUND BARBEN BECK

5 MILES

A walk over the gently undulating hills north-east of Burnsall, with all the attractive scenery one would expect in this beautiful part of Wharfedale. The route describes a high-level circuit of Barben Beck's ravine before descending a splendid old green lane to finish along riverside meadows. A perfect walk for a summer's evening.

Dibble's Bridge   J Keighley

O.S. column
Langerton Hill

Langerton Hill, though of modest height, is reputed to be a good viewpoint. The author cannot verify that, having never been there in anything other than thick mist.

ROUTE DIRECTIONS ① From the village cross the bridge. ② At the far end of the bridge turn L (FP Skuff Rd ½ M) down some steps and follow the river upstream. In the second field go to a ladder-stile about 40 yds from the river and from it head straight up the steep hillside, keeping parallel with a wall on the R. ③ Cross the tarmac lane to a stile opposite (FP Hartlington Raikes Road) and continue straight on uphill to a stile. Across the next field are two stiles. Take the one on the R, in the corner, and bear L across the next field to reach a stile just to the L of two storage tanks. ④ Turn L up the tarmac lane. Just past Raikes Farm, where the lane bends L, take a ladder-stile on the R (SP Pateley Bridge Rd). Follow the wall on the R, crossing two more stiles at field corners. ⑤ From the second of these a short (250yds) wall-side detour L (no right-of-way) leads to the top of Langerton Hill. Return to the stile and turn L. In about 200yds use a ladder-stile to cross to the other side of the wall. When the wall bears slightly L keep straight on down to a stile by a tiny stream. ⑥ Go up to a ladder-stile to the R of a barn, then go up alongside a wall on the R. Pass to the R of the next barn via two ladder-stiles and continue forward, now with the wall on the L. Pass to the L of the farm and along the farm road. ⑦ Turn R along the main road. ⑧ At the far side of the bridge take a stile on the R (FP to Appletreewick 2½M) and bear L away from the beck up over limestone outcrops to a ladder-stile. Maintain direction through a gateway in a wall and on past the LH end of a wall to a ladder-stile. From here descend to a stream. ⑨ Beyond the stream a clear path rises and bears R. It soon curves L and takes a level course along the moor. Avoid any tracks going R down into the ravine. Keep to the level path, parallel with, but at some distance from, the gill. Just past a marker post the path is funnelled between walls to a stile. ⑩ Pass through a short walled section, and at the end of it turn R (footpath sign). Follow the wall on the R. ⑪ On entering a walled lane turn R through a gate onto a stony track (SP Hartlington). Follow this track down to the road (there is a wall on the R nearly all the way). ⑫ Cross the tarmac road to go down

68

the farm road, and at the bottom of it turn R to cross the footbridge. Make for the stile in the far LH corner of the field to reach the riverside path to Burnsall.

DIBBLE'S BRIDGE is a large, solid and not very elegant structure. The extensive repair work to its parapet and adjoining wall bears testimony to the fact that this is a notorious accident blackspot. The most tragic occurred in 1975, when a coach carrying a party of senior citizens went out of control on the long hill down to the bridge from the east. Unable to negotiate the bend, the coach ploughed through the bridge and plunged into the field below.

BARBEN BECK flows for just over three miles from Grimwith Reservoir to the Wharfe, but for the first mile of the way – as far as Dibble's Bridge – it is known as the River Dibb. There is no right-of-way alongside the beck.

Hartlington Hall was built in 1894. During the Second World War the Hall was occupied by the boys of Leeds Grammar School.

Woodhouse Farm, a noble old building, was once a manor-house.

Far Lathe

O.S. MAPS : Landranger Series (1:50 000) Sheet 98
(Wensleydale and Wharfedale)
Outdoor Leisure 10 (1:25 000) Yorkshire Dales
(Southern area)

© Jack Keighley 1990

59

HARD LEVEL GILL & GREAT PINSEAT

5½ MILES

Not a pretty walk – the scenery throughout can only be described as stark, grim and desolate. It will, however, be enjoyed by those walkers whose imagination is stirred by the atmospheric remains of a bygone industry. Although a height of nearly 2000' is reached, the climbing is very gentle on old mining tracks.

Old Gang Smelting Mill

J. Keighley

PARKING At Surrender Bridge, which is on the moorland road running north from Feetham at a junction with another road coming up from Healaugh. (The bridge is not named on the 1:50 000 map). Park on grass by the bridge.
Map ref: 989 999

① ▶ Set off upstream on the wide track (BW only. No vehicles) on the RH side of the beck. ② ▶ About ¼ mile past the ruins of the old smelting mill detour L for about 50yds down to the wall for a good view of Hard Level Force. ③ ▶ When the track forks keep R (straight on). Don't cross the beck. ④ ▶ On passing through a gate the track forks at Level House Bridge. Again keep straight on. Don't cross the beck. The cart track continues, using two fords to cross and re-cross the stream, and just beyond the second ford reaches a gate in the wall on the R. ⑤ ▶ From the gate go straight ahead, climbing gently on a surface of mining spoil. The path soon peters out, but the route is obvious - straight forward along the broad band of mining debris. There are a few small cairns along the way, and eventually you will see ahead of you in the distance a cairn with a tall, upright post. Make for this. ⑥ ▶ To visit the top of Great Pinseat turn L at the cairn with the post and go straight across the heather (no path - beware of hidden bogholes) to the wall. The OS column which marks the summit is on the far side - there is no point in climbing over. Return to the cairn and turn L. The path begins its descent, bearing R to pass to the R of a large and complex sheepfold. After crossing an unpleasant boggy area the path develops into a cart track. Stay on it all the way down to the tarmac road. ⑦ ▶ Turn R along the road. From the parking place at Surrender Bridge a short stroll downstream on a grassy path brings you to the ruins of Surrender Smelting Mill, which are well worth a visit.

GREAT PINSEAT 1914'
O.S column

the old van near the sheepfold

wall
heather
bell pits
Forefield Rake
A cairn with post

spoil
⑥
sheepfold
old van ×
grassy path

ford 9
⑤
spoil
Wetshaw Bottom (a dreary place)

Great Pinseat has many 'bell pits', where early mining of surface lead veins was carried out by 'opencast' methods. Shallow shafts were dug into the vein, and the excavated spoil formed a circular mound. The examples here were probably dug in the mid-eighteenth century, and are now partly filled in and grassed over.

ford
spoil

Flincher Gill
ruin
spoil

Level House Bridge
④
Hard Level Gill
9

WARNING : ALL MINE LEVELS ARE POTENTIALLY DANGEROUS AND SHOULD NOT BE ENTERED

vehicle dump
pond
③
Hard Level Force
②
Old Gang Cave
peat store
level
flue
Old Gang Smelting Mill

stony track

The ford here is the 'watersplash' which features in the 'James Herriot' films

grouse butts

ford
⑦

tarmac road

Hard Level Force, set attractively in a narrow rocky gorge, is the only picturesque place on the walk. There are three caves in the sides of the gorge. Old Gang Cave has a small entrance below a rock face near a small building.

N

condenser (ruin)
flue

Old Gang Beck (or Mill Gill)

THE SMELTING MILLS ARE SCHEDULED ANCIENT MONUMENTS AND ARE BEING CONSERVED. PLEASE DO NOT CLAMBER ON WALLS OR CAUSE ANY DAMAGE

①
Surrender Smelting Mill
Surrender Bridge
to Healaugh and Reeth
to Low Row

70

Hard Level Force

The beck which we follow on the outward half of the walk, and which is here referred to as HARD LEVEL GILL, in fact assumes no fewer than five different names during its five-mile course from the moors to the Swale at Healaugh.

Starting life as FLINCHER GILL, it becomes HARD LEVEL GILL at Level House Bridge. On passing the smelting mill it can't decide whether to be called OLD GANG BECK or MILL GILL, and finally, below Surrender Bridge, it kicks both titles into touch and settles for BARNEY BECK.

THE SMELTING MILLS

The most striking feature of the ruins of the OLD GANG MILL is the well-preserved chimney. The building to which this belonged was used for roasting the lead ore (galena) prior to smelting. The actual smelting took place in the long building next to the path, which had four furnaces. A long pipe, or flue, was constructed to carry away up the hillside, and so disperse, the highly poisonous fumes. The flues which can be seen here joined at some distance up the hill to form one main flue. Above the mill, on the moor, can be seen the stone pillars of the mill's peat store.

SURRENDER MILL was built about 1840 on the site of an earlier building. There were two pairs of ore hearths, set back-to-back (part of one of the furnace arches remains), and set between them would have been the wheel, which worked the bellows and was powered by water brought along a leat from the beck. The two flues can be seen, and the line of the main flue is discernible on the hillside beyond the road.

JUST ABOVE LEVEL HOUSE BRIDGE IS A RUINED BUILDING WITH A FREE-STANDING GABLE END WHICH IS LEANING OMINOUSLY AND SEEMS ON THE POINT OF COLLAPSE. DON'T STAND UNDER IT!

O.S. MAPS : Landranger Series (1:50 000) Sheet 92 (Barnard Castle) (shows all except a tiny section at Surrender Bridge) Outdoor Leisure 30 (1:25 000) Yorkshire Dales (Northern and Central areas)

© Jack Keighley 1990

71

60

BEYOND MALHAM TARN

7½ MILES

Leave the madding crowd behind in the spectacular triangle of country which has The Cove and Gordale Scar as its base, and venture beyond Malham Tarn at its apex into the area known as Malham Moor. The scenery may be tame by comparison with the triangle, but this is fine walking terrain - and you won't have to queue to cross the stiles!

Malham Tarn   J Keighley

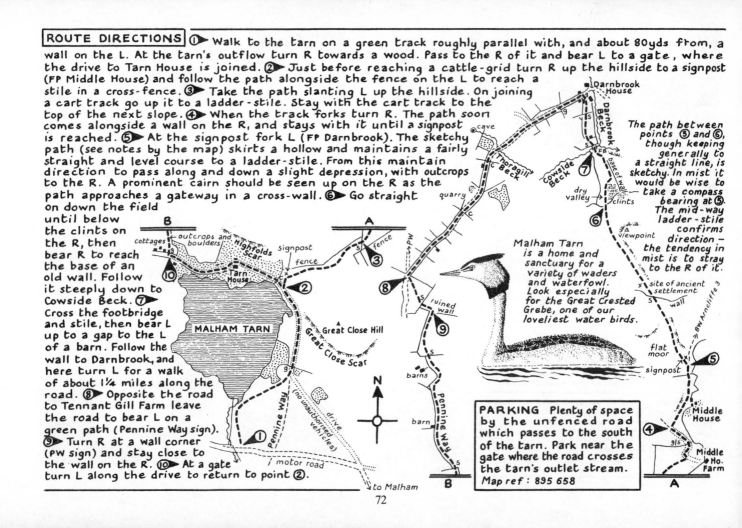

ROUTE DIRECTIONS

① Walk to the tarn on a green track roughly parallel with, and about 80yds from, a wall on the L. At the tarn's outflow turn R towards a wood. Pass to the R of it and bear L to a gate, where the drive to Tarn House is joined. ② Just before reaching a cattle-grid turn R up the hillside to a signpost (FP Middle House) and follow the path alongside the fence on the L to reach a stile in a cross-fence. ③ Take the path slanting L up the hillside. On joining a cart track go up it to a ladder-stile. Stay with the cart track to the top of the next slope. ④ When the track forks turn R. The path soon comes alongside a wall on the R, and stays with it until a signpost is reached. ⑤ At the signpost fork L (FP Darnbrook). The sketchy path (see notes by the map) skirts a hollow and maintains a fairly straight and level course to a ladder-stile. From this maintain direction to pass along and down a slight depression, with outcrops to the R. A prominent cairn should be seen up on the R as the path approaches a gateway in a cross-wall. ⑥ Go straight on down the field until below the clints on the R, then bear R to reach the base of an old wall. Follow it steeply down to Cowside Beck. ⑦ Cross the footbridge and stile, then bear L up to a gap to the L of a barn. Follow the wall to Darnbrook, and here turn L for a walk of about 1¼ miles along the road. ⑧ Opposite the road to Tennant Gill Farm leave the road to bear L on a green path (Pennine Way sign). ⑨ Turn R at a wall corner (PW sign) and stay close to the wall on the R. ⑩ At a gate turn L along the drive to return to point ②.

The path between points ⑤ and ⑥, though keeping generally to a straight line, is sketchy. In mist it would be wise to take a compass bearing at ⑤. The mid-way ladder-stile confirms direction - the tendency in mist is to stray to the R of it.

Malham Tarn is a home and sanctuary for a variety of waders and waterfowl. Look especially for the Great Crested Grebe, one of our loveliest water birds.

PARKING Plenty of space by the unfenced road which passes to the south of the tarn. Park near the gate where the road crosses the tarn's outlet stream. Map ref: 895 658